Southern Kitchen Cookbook

Timeless Southern Cooking Family Recipes

Marie Adams

Copyrights

Disclaimer and Terms of Use

Effort has been made to ensure that the information in this book is accurate and complete. However, the author and the publisher do not warrant the accuracy of the information, text, and graphics contained within the book due to the rapidly changing nature of science, research, known and unknown facts, and internet. The author and the publisher do not hold any responsibility for errors, omissions, or contrary interpretation of the subject matter herein. This book is presented solely for motivational and informational purposes only.

The recipes provided in this book are for informational purposes only and are not intended to provide dietary advice. A medical practitioner should be consulted before making any changes in diet. Additionally, recipe cooking times may require adjustment depending on age and quality of appliances. Readers are strongly urged to take all precautions to ensure ingredients are fully cooked in order to avoid the dangers of foodborne illnesses. The recipes and suggestions provided in this book are solely the opinion of the author. The author and publisher do not take any responsibility for any consequences that may result due to following the instructions provided in this book.

ISBN: 978-1539024200

Printed in the United States

Table of Contents

Introduction

If you enjoy Southern food, this is the perfect cookbook to give your taste buds a delightful kick. After a long stressful day, one is lucky to come home to a peaceful house and a hearty home cooked meal. American Southern food is more than just a cuisine: it is a means of bringing people together. In fact, it is impossible to decide which meal is the most delicious. With its rich, wholesome flavors, American Southern food has a variety of dishes associated with comfort food.

From fried chicken to macaroni and cheese, the southern U.S. is home to some of the most unique foods and has a wide variety of flavors to offer. American Southern food has become integrated with the cultural identity of the South. Whether it is deep fried chicken or barbecued pork, American Southern food is extremely hard to resist.

A bit of history into Soulful Cooking

We are all familiar with foods that are particularly "southern" – fried chicken, jambalaya, collard greens, biscuits, and pecan pie, to name only a few favorites. What many of us don't stop chewing to consider, though, is the complex and unique origin of the food of the South.

All foods develop from a combination of the tastes and traditions of its populations, together with ingredients that are available in the area. Africa, Spain, France, and Scotland have all contributed to the development of Southern food as we think of it today. Each region brought its own ingredients and cooking methods, and combined them with the fresh local foods that are so integral to the cuisine. Corn, rice, and nuts, and of course the varied and plentiful seafood and shellfish of the area, all became central to the diets of the people. The African people brought okra, watermelon, and sweet potatoes. Europeans brought pigs – some of which escaped, becoming the wild hogs of the region today. The natives also taught people what to eat from the local environment, like berries,

"Soul food" is a term used to talk about the food the developed from that of the early African Americans. In the days of slavery, restricting access to the amount and kind of food was used as a way to control the slaves. Their diets mainly consisted of inexpensive foods corn and pork, and poor or leftover cuts of other meat, which they supplemented by growing some of their own crops from home, like okra, peanuts, and sweet potato. These gardens were tended after their work on the plantation was done. Some also fished and hunted for things like possum, rabbits, and squirrels, and they made use of the local ingredients. They used what they could, and "soul food" began to develop.

Preservation methods played their part, as well. Africans didn't know much about preserving meat, because their diets consisted mainly of vegetables and fresh foods. But when enslaved, they had to make every bite count. They learned how to make jerky from the natives, and they began to fry food, as well.

You may be surprised to find that frying food is not a technique that developed in the southern U.S., nor did it originate in Africa. Animals from hot climates don't require fat stores to keep warm. Frying was a method used in northern Europe, and also in North America. Originally, it was a way to preserve the meat. Therefore, you see more fried food from the colder regions of the south, and more smoking, spicing, and pickling in the deep south, where it never really gets cold.

Food became a way to connect with other people, and be comforted. Food has fed the souls of the southern people. It is a way to celebrate life, and preserve family traditions.

With this in mind, we have prepared a superb collection of the best Soulful Southern recipes. Hop aboard the journey where we explore some of the best southern food flavors. And without any further wait, let's get started.

Appetizer Recipes
Southern Sizzling Poppers

Makes: 10 poppers

Ingredients:
10 medium jalapeño peppers
1-1 ½ cups prepared pimento cheese
10 slices bacon
2 tablespoons brown sugar
1 tablespoon barbecue seasoning

Directions:
1. Preheat the oven to 375°F. Line a large baking sheet with parchment paper.
2. Wearing disposable gloves, cut each jalapeño in half down the length of the pepper. Remove the seeds and the white tissue from each of the jalapeño halves.
3. Stuff each jalapeño half with pimento cheese, mounding the cheese slightly above the rim of the pepper.
4. Cut each piece of bacon in half, lengthwise, to create two long, narrow slices. Wrap one slice of bacon around each jalapeño half, overlapping the bacon so most of the pimento cheese is covered. Secure with a toothpick, if needed.
5. Place the stuffed and wrapped jalapeño halves on the baking sheet.
6. Mix together the brown sugar and barbecue spice; sprinkle it evenly over the jalapeños.
7. Bake for 25-35 minutes, or until the bacon is cooked and crisp. Remove from the oven, and allow to stand at least 5 minutes to cool.

Grilled Shrimp and Potato Skewers

Makes: 12 pcs

Ingredients:
12 12 inch skewers
2 pounds small (about 1 ½-inch diameter) red potatoes
2 tablespoons olive oil
2 tablespoons pesto
1 teaspoon salt
1 tablespoon barbecue sauce (a sweet one with brown sugar in it is great)
36 large shrimp (1-1 ½ pounds)
2 bell peppers, seeded and cut into 12 squares each

Directions:
1. If the skewers are wooden, put them in some water to soak.
2. Prick each potato 2 or 3 times with a fork. Put them in a single layer on a large microwave-safe plate. Microwave for 3 minutes.
3. Flip them all over and microwave until fork-tender, 2-4 more minutes.
4. In a small bowl, mix together the olive oil, pesto, salt, and barbecue sauce.
5. Preheat the grill for medium-heat direct grilling.
6. Thread the potatoes, shrimp, and bell peppers onto the skewers, 2 of each item per skewer. Brush all over with the pesto mixture.
7. Grill on the first side for at least 3 minutes, check for doneness, and then turn for the next side.

Spicy Devilled Eggs

Makes: 24 pcs

Ingredients:

1 dozen hard-cooked eggs, peeled
½ cup mayonnaise
3 tablespoons mango chutney
⅛ teaspoon ground red pepper
Kosher salt to taste
Garnish: sliced fresh chives

Directions:

1. Cut the eggs in half lengthwise; carefully remove the yolks and mash them in a bowl.
2. Stir in the mayonnaise, chutney, and red pepper until blended.
3. Spoon the yolk mixture evenly into the egg white halves.
4. Sprinkle evenly with the desired amount of salt.
5. Garnish, if desired. Chill until ready to serve.

Grandma's Crawfish Chowder

Serves: 4

Ingredients:

¾ cup butter, divided
½ bunch green onions, chopped
2 pounds frozen crawfish, cleaned
2 (10.75 ounce) cans condensed cream of potato soup
1 (10.75 ounce) can condensed cream of mushroom soup
1 (15.25 ounce) can whole kernel corn, drained
4 ounces cream cheese, softened
2 cups half-and-half cream
½ teaspoon cayenne pepper

Directions:

1. Melt ¼ cup of butter in a large skillet over medium heat. Sauté the green onions in the butter until tender. Remove them from the pan, and set them aside.
2. In the same skillet, melt ½ cup of butter, and sauté the crawfish for 5 minutes; set it aside.
3. In a large pot over medium heat, combine the potato soup, mushroom soup, corn, and cream cheese. Mix well, and bring it to a slow boil. Stir in the half-and-half, sautéed green onions, and crawfish. Season with cayenne pepper. Bring to a low boil, and simmer 5 minutes to blend the flavors.

Southern Crispy Fried Green Tomatoes

Serves: 4-8

Ingredients:
4 large green tomatoes
2 eggs
½ cup milk
1 cup all-purpose flour
2 teaspoons sea salt
½ teaspoon cayenne powder
½ cup cornmeal
½ cup bread crumbs
1 quart vegetable oil for frying

Directions:
1. Slice the tomatoes in ½-inch thick slices. Discard the tops and bottoms.
2. Combine and whisk the eggs and milk together in a medium-size bowl.
3. Set up your dredging station, with one bowl for flour, salt, and cayenne powder, and in another, combine the cornmeal and bread crumbs.
4. Dip your tomatoes into the egg mixture, and roll them in the flour.
5. Dip again in the egg, and cover with crushed bread crumbs and cornmeal.
6. Pour the vegetable oil into a large saucepan, and heat over medium heat.
7. Working in batches, deep fry the tomatoes until they are golden brown. Remove them carefully from the hot oil with a slotted spoon, and set them aside on paper towel to drain.

Fried Shrimp

Makes 6 servings

Ingredients
3 cups of large, deveined and peeled shrimp
Salt and pepper
1 egg, beaten
½ cup yellow cornmeal
½ teaspoon baking powder
½ cup half and half cream
½ cup buttermilk
1 teaspoons salt
¼ teaspoon black pepper
½ teaspoon baking powder
½ teaspoon all-purpose flour
Oil to fry your shrimp
¼ teaspoon pepper

Directions
1. Start by seasoning generously your shrimp with some salt and pepper and then leave them to sit at room temperature for 10 to 15 minutes.
2. Combine the eggs, cornmeal, baking powder, cream, buttermilk, salt, pepper, baking powder and flour together in a mixing bowl and mix until well blended and smooth.
3. Heat the oil in the deep fryer until it reaches 350°F.
4. Dip the shrimp in the batter to coat evenly.
5. Fry the shrimp until they are golden. This will take around 2 minutes.
6. Serve the shrimp hot, with your favorite sauce.

Corn Chowder

Makes 10 to 12 Servings

Ingredients
4 ounces chopped bacon
½ cup celery, finely chopped
½ cup carrots, finely chopped
1 cup onions, finely chopped
2 tablespoons garlic, minced
¼ cup all-purpose flour
2 quarts chicken stock
1 ½ cups russet potatoes, cubed and peeled
1 cup heavy cream
5 cups kernel corn
¾ cup red bell peppers, finely chopped
1 tablespoon salt
¼ teaspoon cayenne pepper
Finely chopped parsley for garnishing

Directions
1. Place an 8-quart stockpot over medium heat and allow the bacon to cook until it is crispy. This should take about 5 minutes.
2. When the bacon is cooked, remove it to drain on a paper towel.
3. To the stockpot, add the onions, carrots, and celery and allow the mixture to cook, stirring occasionally, it until it is soft, about 5 minutes.
4. Add garlic, bell peppers, and corn to the pot and allow cook for 10 minutes, stirring often.

5. Sprinkle the flour over the vegetables, and stir constantly for 5 minutes. Slowly pour in the chicken stock, mixing to combine all the ingredients. You may use a whisk if necessary to break up the lumps if any have formed.
6. Add the potatoes and bring the mixture to a boil, and cook for at least 20 minutes, until the potatoes are fork tender.
7. Finally, add salt, cayenne pepper, and stir in the cream.
8. Garnish with some bacon and fresh parsley. Enjoy!

Hot Corn Dip

Makes 10 servings

Ingredients
2 cups corn kernel
½ cup diced onion
2 tablespoons mayonnaise
1 ½ tablespoons butter
1 clove garlic, minced
1-2 jalapenos, seeded and diced
¼ teaspoon seasoned salt
¾ cup sharp cheddar cheese, shredded
½ cup Monterey Jack Cheese, shredded
¼ teaspoon chili powder
4 tablespoons cream cheese
1 green onion, sliced
Tortilla chips for dipping
Cooking spray

Directions
1. Preheat oven to 375°F.
2. In a skillet, melt butter, and add corn, onion, and jalapeño. Sauté for 3 minutes.
3. Add garlic and continue to sauté for 1 to 2 more minutes.
4. Remove the mixture from heat and allow the mixture to cool for a few minutes before adding all the remaining ingredients. Stir to combine.
5. Transfer to a baking dish coated with cooking spray, and bake for 20 minutes, until the cheese bubbles.
6. Serve with tortilla chips for dipping.

Crab Cakes

Makes 4 servings

Ingredients
½ cup mayonnaise
1 large egg, lightly beaten
1 tablespoon Dijon mustard
1 tablespoon Worcestershire sauce
½ tablespoon hot sauce
1 pound fresh lump crabmeat, drained
1 cup crushed saltines (20 crackers)
1 quart vegetable oil
Tartar sauce (to serve)

Directions
1. Line a baking sheet with waxed paper.
2. In a mixing bowl, stir the mayonnaise, egg, mustard, Worcestershire sauce and hot sauce together.
3. Fold in the crabmeat and the saltines, and allow the mixture to rest for 5 minutes.
4. Shape the mixture into 8 patties, and place them on the baking sheet, cover, and chill for an hour.
5. Heat a few tablespoons of oil in a frying pan, and fry the crab cakes over medium heat for 3 to 4 minutes on each side until golden.
6. Place the fried patties on paper towels to allow the oil to drain.
7. Serve the crab cakes while they are still hot along with tartar sauce, if desired.

Southern Pimento Cheese

Makes 12 Servings

Ingredients
2 cups shredded cheddar cheese
½ cup mayonnaise
¼ teaspoon garlic powder
¼ teaspoon ground cayenne powder
8 ounces cream cheese
1 jalapeno pepper, minced
½ teaspoon onion powder
1 jar diced pimentos, drained
Salt and pepper to taste
Crackers or baguette, to serve

Directions
1. In the bowl of a mixer, place the mayonnaise, garlic powder, onion powder, cheddar cheese, cream cheese, cayenne pepper, pimentos, and jalapeño.
2. Mix all the ingredients at medium speed until thoroughly combined.
3. Season the mixture with salt and pepper, and transfer to a clean bowl.
4. Serve the pimento cheese with crackers or slices of baguette.

Note: pimento cheese is also great in hamburgers!

Coconut Shrimp

Makes 6-8 servings

Ingredients
1 cup flour
2 pounds large shrimp
½ teaspoon salt
½ teaspoon sugar
1 egg, lightly beaten
2 tablespoons vegetable oil
2/3 cup grated coconut
1 ½ teaspoon curry powder
1 cup ice water
Hot sauce, for serving

Directions
1. Shell and devein the shrimp, leaving the tail intact.
2. In a medium sized bowl, combine the egg, sugar, salt, vegetable oil, ice water, and flour, and beat the mixture until it is smooth.
3. In a separate bowl, mix together the coconut and curry powder.
4. Dip the shrimp into the batter and then into the coconut mixture.
5. Fry the coconut shrimp in hot fat until it turns golden brown on both sides.
6. Serve the shrimp with some hot sauce, if desired.

Deep Fried Dill Pickles

Makes 12 servings

Ingredients
2 large eggs
1 cup buttermilk
½ teaspoon hot sauce
1 ½ teaspoons black pepper, separated
1 ¼ teaspoons salt, separated
2 ¼ cups all-purpose flour, separated
1 cup corn meal
1 teaspoon cayenne pepper
1 jar dill pickle slices
Vegetable oil for frying
Ranch dressing, or your choice of dip, to serve

Directions
1. In a medium sized bowl, combine the eggs, buttermilk, hot sauce, ¼ cup flour, black pepper, cayenne pepper, and ¼ teaspoon of salt.
2. In another shallow bowl, combine the remaining 2 cups of flour, cornmeal, and the remaining 1 teaspoon of salt and black pepper.
3. Preheat the oil in the deep fryer to 375°F.
4. Remove the pickle slices from the jar and blot them dry with a paper towel.
5. Dip the pickle slices first into the buttermilk mixture and then in the cornmeal mixture.
6. Deep fry the pickles until they appear golden brown, this will take 1 to 2 minutes.
7. Drain the deep fried pickles on a paper towel to get rid of the excess oil.
8. Serve with a dish of ranch dressing for dipping.

9. Fry the shrimp until they turn lightly golden, about one minute.
10. Drain the shrimp on a paper towel.
11. Coat the shrimp with the sauces, and serve with chopped scallions to garnish.

Pineapple Cream Cheese Salad

Makes 6-8 servings

Ingredients
½ cup mayonnaise
1 cup whipped cream
1 package lemon gelatin
1 can crushed pineapple
1 cup cream cheese
1 cup water
⅓ cup chopped walnuts

Directions
1. In a medium sized bowl combine the whipped cream and mayonnaise together and then place in the refrigerator. Allow the mixture to cool for an hour.
2. Combine the pineapple and water in a saucepan and bring to a boil. Reduce heat to low.
3. Add the lemon gelatin to the mixture, stir continuously until dissolved completely, and then allow it to cool.
4. Before the gelatin sets, add the whipped cream mixture together with the cream cheese. Stir to combine well. Place in the refrigerator for 1-2 hours, or until set.
5. Sprinkle the walnuts on top. Serve chilled.

Chicken and Turkey Recipes
Grandma's Southern Fried Chicken

Serves: 10

Ingredients:
2 pounds chicken cuts (any parts)
2 tablespoons seasoned salt
1 tablespoon black pepper
2 quarts oil for frying
Hot sauce, for serving

For the coating:
1 cup all-purpose flour
1 tablespoon garlic powder
1 teaspoon onion powder
1 teaspoon paprika
1 teaspoon Italian seasoning
½ teaspoon chili powder SOUTHERN
½ teaspoon sugar
3 teaspoons seasoning salt
⅛ teaspoon poultry seasoning
1 ¼ teaspoons black pepper
¼ teaspoon ground cayenne red pepper powder
¼ teaspoon thyme, crush between your fingers when adding
¼ teaspoon basil

Directions:
1. Prepare a baking tray with a sheet of waxed paper.
2. Rinse the chicken pieces thoroughly, pat them dry with paper towel, and sprinkle with seasoned salt and pepper. Set them aside.
3. In a doubled brown paper lunch sack, mix together all of the coating ingredients.

4. One piece at a time, place the chicken in the bag. Shake well until thoroughly coated. Shake off any excess, and place them on the waxed paper for 15 minutes, or until they are dry.
5. Heat the oil in a large saucepan over medium-high heat, and keep it between 350°F and 375°F.
6. When the chicken has absorbed all the seasoning, fry it in small batches until it is golden brown and cooked through.
7. Serve with hot sauce!

Classic Southern Chicken and Dumplings

Serves: 8-10

Ingredients
1 whole chicken
½ teaspoon dried thyme
½ teaspoon garlic powder
1 teaspoon chicken bouillon granules
1 cup milk
1 teaspoon bacon drippings
3 cups self-rising flour
1½ teaspoons of salt, separated
¾ teaspoon pepper
½ tablespoon poultry seasoning
⅓ cup shortening
Water

Directions
1. Place the chicken in a Dutch oven, and sprinkle with, garlic powder, thyme, ½ teaspoon of salt, ½ teaspoon of pepper. Fill halfway with water and bring it to a boil.
2. Cover with the lid, and reduce the heat to medium low, allow it to simmer for at least an hour.
3. Remove the chicken to a platter, but reserve the broth.
4. Allow the chicken to cool for 30 minutes, then remove the skin and bone and shred the meat into small pieces.
5. Skim the fat from the broth. Put the shredded chicken back into the pot, and add 1 teaspoon of salt, ¼ teaspoon of pepper, and bouillon granules. Simmer the mixture while preparing the dumplings.

6. In a bowl, combine the flour and poultry seasoning. Cut the shortening and bacon drippings with a pastry blender until crumbly. Stir in the milk until the dough forms a ball. Do not overmix.
7. Turn the dough out onto a lightly floured surface. Roll to ⅛ inch thickness, and cut it into 1 inch pieces.
8. Slowly, drop the dumplings in to the simmering broth, stirring it gently. Cover and simmer for 25 minutes.
9. Serve in a large serving dish.

Old Fashioned Chicken and Vegetable Roast

Serves: 8

Ingredients:
2 tablespoons olive oil
1 large sweet onion, peeled and quartered
1 pound carrots, peeled and cut into 2-inch pieces
5-6 potatoes, peeled and quartered
3 pounds pot roast
1 cup dry red wine or water
4 cups beef stock
3 bay leaves
1 teaspoon thyme
1 teaspoon rosemary

Directions:
1. Preheat the oven to 275°F.
2. Place a Dutch oven over medium-high heat, and add 2 tablespoons of olive oil. Brown the onion until soft. Remove it from the pan and brown the carrots. Remove the carrots, and lightly brown the potatoes.
3. Remove the potatoes and add a bit more oil to the pot, if necessary. Increase the heat to high, and sear the pot roast on all sides for a minute or two.
4. Remove the beef from the pan. Slowly add 1 cup of dry red wine, stirring to deglaze the pan. Put the meat back in, and place the vegetables around the edges of the meat. Pour the 4 cups of beef broth into the pan, so the meat is halfway immersed.
5. Cover the pot, put it in the oven, and bake for 3 to 4 hours, until the meat is very tender and the vegetables are cooked through. Let the meat sit for a few minutes before slicing and serving.

Chicken Divan

Serves: 4

Ingredients:
2 ½ cups broccoli, chopped and cooked
2 cups chicken meat, cooked and shredded
2 (4 ½ ounce) cans mushrooms, drained
2 (10.75 ounce) cans condensed cream of chicken soup
1 cup mayonnaise
1 ½ teaspoons lemon juice
¼ teaspoon curry powder
¼ teaspoon paprika
½ teaspoon black pepper
1 tablespoon melted butter
½ cup shredded Cheddar cheese

Directions:
1. Preheat the oven to 350°F. Grease a 3-quart casserole dish.
2. Arrange the cooked broccoli in the prepared baking dish, and place the chicken over the broccoli. Add the mushrooms.
3. In a medium bowl, combine the soup, mayonnaise, lemon juice, curry powder, paprika, pepper, and melted butter. Mix them together, and pour the sauce mixture over the chicken and vegetables.
4. Sprinkle the cheese on top, and bake in the preheated oven until the casserole is bubbly and the cheese is golden brown, 30-45 minutes.

Southern Chicken Fried Steak

Makes 6 servings

Ingredients
2 cups all-purpose flour
6 small skinless and boneless chicken breasts
¼ cup oil for frying
1 teaspoon dry oregano
½ teaspoon cumin
½ teaspoon paprika
1-2 pinches cayenne pepper, to taste
Salt and pepper to taste
2 eggs
Hot sauce for serving

Directions
1. In a large bowl, combine the flour with the oregano, cumin, paprika, cayenne, salt, and pepper.
2. In another bowl, beat the eggs.
3. Between 2 plastic wrap paper, pound each chicken breast until you get them to about ½ inch thick. Try to make the cutlets even in size.
4. Coat each chicken cutlet first in the flour mixture, then dip into egg, followed by another coat in the flour mixture.
5. In a skillet, heat oil over medium high heat. Place veal cutlets into hot oil and fry until each side is browned, about 5 minutes per side.
6. Serve with a side of hot sauce.

King Ranch Chicken Casserole

Makes 8 servings

Ingredients

2 cups cooked chicken, chopped
2 tablespoons vegetable oil
1 large onion, chopped
1 large green bell pepper, chopped
¼ teaspoon black pepper
¼ teaspoon salt
¼ teaspoon garlic powder
1 can cream of mushroom soup (10 ¾ ounce)
1 can diced tomatoes with green chilies (10 ounce)
12 corn tortillas (6 inch)
2 cups cheddar cheese, shredded

Directions

1. Heat the oil in a large skillet over medium high heat, and sauté the onions and bell pepper until tender.
2. Stir in the chicken, salt, black pepper, garlic powder, mushroom soup, and tomatoes, and remove from the heat.
3. Lightly grease a 13x9 inch baking dish. Tear in the tortillas into 1 inch pieces and layer ⅓ of the tortillas in the bottom of the baking dish.
4. Top the layer of tortillas with ⅓ of the chicken mixture, then with 2/3 cup cheese. Repeat layers twice.
5. Bake the dish in the oven at 350°F for 30 to 35 minutes.
6. Let the casserole rest for 10 minutes before serving.

Plantation Chicken Pot Pie

Serves: 8

Ingredients:

3 medium red potatoes, washed but unpeeled
1 large carrot, trimmed and diced
½ cup frozen peas
6 tablespoons salted butter
6 tablespoons all-purpose flour
2 cups chicken broth or stock
½ teaspoon salt
½ teaspoon black pepper
1 teaspoon dried rosemary, crushed
1 teaspoon dried thyme, crushed
1 ½ cups half-and-half
1 pound boneless, skinless chicken breasts or mixed chicken pieces (about 2 ½ cups cubed), cooked
2 homemade pie crusts, or store-bought refrigerated pie crusts, softened to room temperature

Directions:

1. Preheat the oven to 425°F. Chop the potatoes into small cubes and place them in a microwave safe dish. Cook on high for about 2 ½ minutes, or until tender. Set them aside.
2. In another microwave safe dish, combine the carrots and peas. Microwave on high for about 2 minutes, or until tender. Add them to the potatoes.
3. In a large skillet, melt the butter over medium heat. Add the flour one tablespoon at a time, stirring well before adding the next. Cook, stirring constantly, until the mixture is bubbly and there are no remaining lumps, about 5 minutes. Slowly begin to incorporate

the chicken stock, stirring vigorously until fully incorporated.

4. Remove the pot from the heat, add the salt, pepper, rosemary, and thyme. Stir in the half-and-half until smooth.

5. Stir the chicken into the cream mixture, then add the potatoes, carrots, and peas; mix well. Taste and adjust the seasonings as needed.

6. Unroll one of the pie crusts and place it in a 9-inch, ungreased deep dish, glass pie plate. Gently press the crust down into the bottom and edges of the pie plate. Pour the hot filling into the crust and top with the remaining crust, tucking the top crust in under the edges of the bottom crust. Flute the edges and cut vents into the top of the crust.

7. Bake immediately at 425°F for 15 minutes. Remove the pie from the oven and place strips of foil around the edges of the crust to prevent over-browning. Return it to oven for an additional 15-25 minutes, or until the crust is golden brown and the filling is bubbling. Let it stand for 5 minutes before cutting.

Southern Roasted Turkey

Serves: 10

Ingredients:

1 16 pound fresh turkey, neck, tail, and giblets reserved for the gravy
⅔ cup unsalted butter, softened
3 ½ teaspoons sea salt, divided
2 ½ teaspoon freshly ground black pepper, divided
2 tablespoons paprika (hot or sweet)
2 tablespoons finely chopped fresh thyme
4 teaspoons garlic, minced
¾ teaspoon cayenne powder
¼ teaspoon poultry seasoning

Directions:

1. Line a 12x16 heavy duty roasting pan with 2 layers of paper towels. Rinse and blot the turkey dry inside and out.
2. In a small bowl, combine the butter with 2 teaspoons salt and 1 teaspoon pepper. Stir in the paprika, thyme, garlic, cayenne, and poultry seasoning. Set aside ¼ cup of the butter mixture to use when you are making the gravy.
3. Slide your hand under the turkey's skin to loosen it from the breast and thigh meat. Using your fingers, spread the butter directly on the breast and thigh meat, being careful not to tear the skin. Season the turkey inside and out with 1 ½ teaspoons each salt and pepper.

4. Tuck the wings behind the neck and tie the legs together with kitchen twine. Set the turkey breast-side up in the prepared pan. Cover it loosely with waxed paper or parchment, and refrigerate for 1-2 days. Uncover the turkey, discard the paper towels, and set the turkey on a V-rack in the roasting pan.
5. Let it sit for 1 hour at room temperature. Position a rack in the lower third of the oven and heat the oven to 350°F.
6. Roast the turkey, basting occasionally after 1 hour, and rotating the pan halfway through, until an instant-read thermometer inserted into the thickest part of the thigh registers 165°F, about 2-2 ½ hours. If the skin gets too dark during roasting, tent with foil. Tilt the turkey so the juice in the cavity runs into the roasting pan.
7. Transfer the turkey to a platter or carving board. Remove the string, tent with foil, and let it rest at room temperature for at least 30 minutes (and up to 1 hour) before carving and serving.

Traditional Jambalaya

Makes 4 servings

Ingredients
1 pound chicken breast, diced
1 medium sized yellow onion, chopped
2 tablespoons butter
½ pound andouille sausage, sliced in ¼ inch slices
1 green bell pepper, diced
1 stalk celery, diced
3 cloves of garlic, minced
2 teaspoons hot sauce
2 cups chicken broth
1 teaspoon Worcestershire sauce
1 can diced tomatoes
2 bay leaves
¾ teaspoon salt
½ teaspoon black pepper each
½ pound raw shrimp, deveined
2 tablespoons Creole seasoning
1 cup long grain rice
4 green onions, thinly sliced, for garnish

Directions
1. Combine all the spices for the Creole seasoning and place in a clean coffee grinder. Grind until you have a fine powder, and store the powder in an airtight jar.
2. Place the chicken in a large bowl and sprinkle with 1 tablespoon of the Creole seasoning. Set it aside to rest.
3. Place a large skillet on medium high heat and melt the butter.
4. Cook the chicken and the sausage until browned, and drain excess fat.

5. Add the bell pepper, garlic, onion, and celery, and cook for 4 minutes.
6. Add the rice, and the remaining tablespoon of Creole seasoning, diced tomatoes, hot sauce, salt, black pepper, and Worcestershire sauce, and stir the mixture until it is thoroughly combined.
7. Add the chicken broth and bay leaves, and bring the mixture to a boil. Reduce the heat to medium low, cover the pot, and allow it to simmer for 15 minutes. Give it a stir around the halfway point.
8. Finally, add the shrimp, cover, and then allow the Jambalaya to simmer for another 10 minutes until the rice turns tender and thoroughly cooked.
9. Place in a serving dish and enjoy with a sprinkle of green onions, while it is still hot!

Buttermilk Fried Chicken

Serves: 6

Ingredients:
2 cups buttermilk
1 tablespoon Dijon mustard
1 teaspoon salt
1 teaspoon ground black pepper
1 teaspoon cayenne pepper
½ teaspoon paprika
1 whole chicken, cut into pieces
2 cups all-purpose flour
1 tablespoon baking powder
1 tablespoon garlic powder
1 tablespoon onion powder
5 cups vegetable oil for frying

Directions:
1. In a medium bowl, combine the buttermilk, mustard, salt, pepper, cayenne, and paprika, and pour the mixture into a re-sealable plastic bag. Add the chicken pieces, squeeze out any excess air, and seal the bag. Marinate in the refrigerator for 2-8 hours, turning occasionally so the pieces are well coated with the marinade.
2. Before cooking, combine the flour, baking powder, garlic powder, and onion powder in a separate large plastic bag. Shake to mix thoroughly. Working one piece at a time, transfer the chicken into the dry ingredients, and shake well to cover them completely. After all chicken pieces are coated, repeat the process by dipping them in the buttermilk marinade and shaking them in the dry coating again.

3. Heat the oil in a large frying pan or Dutch oven over medium-high heat, keeping it below the smoke point. When the oil is hot, fry the chicken in batches. Turn frequently until each piece is golden brown and the juices run clear.

Deep-fried Turkey

Serves: 10

Ingredients:
6 quarts hot water
1 pound sea salt
1 pound dark brown sugar
5 pounds ice
1 (13-14 pound) turkey, with giblets removed
5 cups peanut oil

Directions:
1. Place the hot water, salt, and brown sugar in an upright, 5-gallon drink cooler and stir until the salt and sugar dissolve completely. Add the ice and stir until the mixture is cool. Immerse the turkey in the brine, weighing it down if necessary. Put on the lid, and keep it in a cool, dry place for 8 to 16 hours.
2. Remove the turkey from the brine, rinse it, and pat it dry. Allow it to sit at room temperature for at least 30 minutes before cooking. Set it in a wire basket that fits inside your pot.
3. Pour the peanut oil into a 30-quart pot over high heat on an outside propane burner with a sturdy structure. Bring the temperature of the oil to 250°F. Once the oil has come to temperature, carefully lower the bird into the oil and bring the temperature up to 350°F. Reduce the flame in order to keep the temperature at 350°F.
4. After 35 minutes, gently lift the turkey out of the oil and let it drain a little. Check the temperature of the turkey using a probe thermometer.
5. Once the turkey breast temperature reaches 160°F, carefully lift it out of the oil, and allow it to rest for a minimum of 30 minutes. The bird will reach an internal temperature of 165-170°F as the heat and juices inside the meat equalizes.

Kentucky Hot Browns

Makes 4 servings

Ingredients
4 thick white bread slices
12 ounces sliced roasted turkey
2 tomatoes, sliced
8 bacon slices, cooked
1 cup shredded Parmesan cheese
Mornay Sauce (recipe follows)

Directions
1. Preheat broiler and place oven rack on the upper position at about 6 inches from heat source.
2. On a baking dish, place bread slices and broil until golden brown on each side, about 1 minute per side.
3. Arrange bread slices on 4 lightly greased individual baking dishes, and top with turkey slices.
4. Pour warm Mornay sauce over the turkey, and sprinkle each evenly with the Parmesan cheese.
5. Place under the broiler until the cheese is melted and golden, about 2-4 minutes.
6. Top with tomato slices and bacon, and serve.

Mornay Sauce

Yields approx.1 ½ cups

Ingredients
½ cup butter
⅓ cup all-purpose flour
1 ½ cups milk
¼ teaspoon salt
¼ teaspoon pepper
½ cup shredded Parmesan

Directions
1. Melt butter in a saucepan over medium- high heat.
2. Whisk in flour, and cook for 1 minute, whisking constantly.
3. Add milk and bring it to a boil. Reduce heat to medium-low, and continue cooking until it has thickened, about 3-4 minutes.
4. Whisk in Parmesan cheese, salt and pepper. Continue stirring until the cheese is melted. Serve immediately.

Beef Recipes

Chunky Beef Chili

Yields about 9 Cups

Ingredients
4 pounds boneless chuck roast, cubed
2 6 oz. cans of tomato paste
2 15 oz. cans tomato sauce
2 tablespoons chili powder
2 teaspoons granulated garlic
1 teaspoon ground cumin
1 teaspoon ground oregano
1 teaspoon salt
½ teaspoon onion powder
½ teaspoon ground black pepper
¼ teaspoon ground red pepper
1 teaspoon paprika

<u>For Topping</u>
Chopped onions
Crushed tortilla chips
Shredded cheese
Sour cream

Directions
1. Brown the meat in batches in a Dutch oven over medium high heat.
2. Remove the meat from the pot, but keep the drippings in the pot. Add chili powder and cook for 2 minutes, stirring constantly.

3. Place the beef back in the pot, and add the tomato paste with the tomato sauce, oregano, cumin, paprika, black pepper, red pepper, salt, onion powder, and granulated garlic. Stir well.
4. Bring the mixture to a boil, reduce the heat to low and allow it to simmer, uncovered for 1 ½ hours, stirring occasionally. Serve hot, garnished with toppings.

Sunday Night Pot Roast

Makes 6 to 8 servings

Ingredients
1 boneless bottom round roast (3 to 4 pounds)
¼ cup vegetable oil
2 yellow onions, peeled and quartered
3 cloves garlic, crushed
2 cups beef broth
2 bay leaves
2 fresh thyme sprigs
3 carrots, sliced into ½ inch pieces
1 cup red wine
1 tablespoon tomato paste
Kosher salt and black pepper to taste
Fresh parsley leaves, chopped

Directions
1. Preheat oven to 350°F.
2. Season the roast with both sides with salt and pepper.
3. Heat oil in a Dutch oven over medium high heat and sear the roast on both sides. Remove the roast from the pot and set aside.
4. Combine the tomato paste, garlic, onions in the pot, and allow the mixture to cook until it has colored.
5. Add the thyme, bay leaves, broth, and wine, and place the roast in the liquid.
6. Bring the mixture to a simmer, then cover and place in the oven.
7. Allow the pot to roast for 1 ½ hours, and then add the carrots. Cook for another hour.

8. Transfer the roast to a cutting board and allow it to rest for 10 to 20 minutes before carving.
9. Skim the fat from the braising liquid, and serve it piping hot over the meat, with freshly chopped parsley.

Southern Beef Tenderloin

Serves: 6

Ingredients:

Marinade
1 cup soy sauce
⅔ cup vegetable oil
3 tablespoons brown sugar
2 tablespoons Dijon mustard
1 tablespoon Worcestershire sauce
1 tablespoon white vinegar
1 teaspoon garlic powder
½ teaspoon cayenne powder
1 green onion, chopped

Other ingredients
1 (5-6 pounds) beef tenderloin
Horseradish sauce, for serving

Directions:
1. Combine all the marinade ingredients, and place the mixture in a large re-sealable bag. Place the tenderloin in the bag, and turn to coat. Refrigerate for 3-5 days, turning occasionally.
2. Preheat the oven to 400°F. Place the tenderloin on shallow roasting rack and bake for 40-55 minutes, until the desired doneness is reached. (A meat thermometer reads 145° for medium rare, or 160° for medium.)
3. Let the meat stand for 10 minutes before slicing. Serve with horseradish sauce for dipping.

Heart-Warming Southern Beef Stew

Serves: 4

Ingredients:
1 tablespoon butter
1 ½ pounds beef stew meat, cut into ½-inch pieces
1 (10 ounce) can diced tomatoes and green chillies
3 (14 ½ ounce) cans stewed, diced tomatoes
1 (10 ounce) package frozen cut okra
1 (10 ounce) package frozen baby lima beans
1 (10 ounce) package frozen corn kernels
4 medium potatoes, peeled and diced

Directions:
1. Melt the butter in a Dutch oven over medium-high heat. Add the beef, and quickly brown it on all sides.
2. Pour in the diced tomatoes with green chilies, and stewed tomatoes. Add the okra, lima beans, and corn.
3. Bring it to a boil, and reduce the heat to medium.
4. Simmer for about 1 hour. Add the potatoes, and continue to simmer for another 30 minutes, or until the meat is very tender.

Old-South Meatloaf

Serves: 4-5

Ingredients:
1 ½ pounds ground beef
1 egg, lightly beaten
1 onion, diced
1 cup milk
1 cup dried bread crumbs
1 teaspoon red pepper flakes
1 teaspoon salt
½ teaspoon freshly ground black pepper

For the topping:
2 tablespoons brown sugar
1 tablespoon ground mustard
⅓ cup ketchup

Directions:
1. Half an hour before beginning to prepare the meatloaf, set out the ground beef and let it come to room temperature.
2. Preheat the oven to 350°F.
3. In a large bowl, combine all the ingredients for the meatloaf. Press the mixture into a 9x5 loaf pan, or into lightly greased muffin cups.
4. Bake for 45 minutes if you're using a loaf pan, 25 if you're using muffin cups. Take it out and drain away any grease.
5. In a small mixing bowl, combine the brown sugar, mustard, and ketchup. Mix well and spread it on top of the meatloaf.

6. Return the pan or tray to the oven, and bake for another few minutes until the topping is hot, and the internal temperature is 155°F.
7. Tent some foil over the meatloaf, and let it sit for 10 minutes before serving.

Peggy's Scrumptious Hamburger Casserole

Serves: 5

Ingredients:
1 pound hamburger
1 medium onion, chopped
8 ounces button mushrooms, sliced
Salt and pepper, to taste
½ cup water
1 (15 ½ ounce) can green beans, drained
1 (16 ounce) carton cottage cheese
1 ½ cups crushed soda crackers
3 tablespoons cold butter, cut in ½-inch cubes

Directions:
1. Preheat the oven to 350°F, and prepare a casserole dish with cooking spray.
2. Brown the hamburger in large skillet over medium heat. When it is almost cooked through, drain away any grease and increase the heat to medium-high. Add the onion and mushrooms and cook, stirring occasionally, until the meat and vegetables are nicely browned. Season with salt and pepper.
3. Pour in the water and stir. Allow the liquid to reduce for 1-2 minutes before stirring in the beans and cottage cheese.
4. Transfer the casserole to the prepared casserole dish. Cover top with crackers and pats of butter. Bake for about 40 minutes, or until the top is brown.

Timeless Sloppy-Joes

Serves: 4

Ingredients:

For the coleslaw:
⅓ cup mayonnaise
⅓ cup sour cream
1 tablespoon apple cider vinegar
½ teaspoon sea salt, divided
¼ teaspoon black pepper
¼ teaspoon celery seed
1 (16 ounce) package coleslaw mix

For the filling:
1 pound ground sirloin
1 teaspoon salt
½ teaspoon red pepper flakes
2 tablespoons steak sauce
1 (16 ounce) can chili, warmed

4 hamburger buns, toasted

Directions:

1. Preheat the grill to 375°F, or medium-high heat.
2. Whisk together the mayonnaise, sour cream, apple cider vinegar, salt, pepper, and celery seed in a large bowl. Add the coleslaw mix and toss to coat. Cover and chill until ready to serve.
3. Combine the ground sirloin, steak sauce, salt and red pepper flakes. Gently shape the mixture into 4 patties, 4 inches wide.
4. Grill the patties for 4-5 minutes on each side, or until the beef is no longer pink in the middle. Serve on hamburger buns, and top the burgers with the coleslaw mixture and a spoonful of warm chili.

Beefy Bell Pepper Surprise

Serves: 6

Ingredients:
6 large green bell peppers
3 tablespoons olive oil
2 cups ground beef
1 onion, diced
1 jalapeño pepper, seeded and minced
1 clove garlic, minced
½ teaspoon oregano
1 tablespoon Creole seasoning
½ teaspoon black pepper
1 cup white rice, uncooked
2 ½ cups chicken broth
8 ounces canned tomato sauce
Juice of 1 lime
Hot sauce to taste, optional
1 cup cheddar, shredded

Directions:
1. Preheat the oven to 325°F, and prepare a 9x13 baking dish with cooking spray.
2. Remove the tops and seeds from the bell peppers, and blanch them in boiling water for 3 minutes. Drain them well, and dry with paper towels.
3. Heat the oil in a deep skillet over medium heat. Sauté the beef until it is browned, and drain any excess fat. Add the onion, jalapeño, garlic, oregano, Creole seasoning, and pepper, and hot sauce, if using. Squeeze the lime juice over the mixture. Cook for 5 minutes to allow the flavors to develop.

4. Stir in the rice and cook for 1 minute before adding the chicken broth and tomato sauce. Fill the peppers with the mixture and arrange them in the baking dish. Divide the cheddar among the peppers, pressing gently into the surface of the meat mixture so it doesn't slide off while melting.
5. Bake for 15-20 minutes. Serve with salad and garlic bread.

Pork Recipes

Roasted Pork with Onion Gravy

Serves: 6

Ingredients:
2 tablespoons cornstarch
1 (14 ½ ounce) can beef broth
1 clove garlic, minced
¼ teaspoon black pepper
¼ teaspoon salt
2 tablespoons butter
6 pork chops, ½-inch thick
2 onions, thinly sliced

Directions:
1. Mix the cornstarch with the broth until smooth, and set it aside.
2. Melt the butter in a large skillet over medium heat.
3. Season the pork chops with salt and pepper, and cook them for 5 minutes on each side, or until they are nicely browned. Remove them from the heat and set them aside, covered.
4. Add the onion and garlic to the pan and cook over medium heat, until the onion is translucent but still crisp. Stir the cornstarch mixture and add it to skillet. Cook until it comes to a boil and thickens, stirring constantly.
5. Return the chops to pan, cover, and cook over low heat for 15 minutes, or until the chops are done and tender.

Low Country Slow Cooker Pulled Pork

Serves: 4-6

Ingredients:
1 tablespoon butter
2 pounds boneless pork roast
1 tablespoon Cajun seasoning
1 tablespoon brown sugar
½ teaspoon black pepper
1 medium onion, chopped
8 ounces mushrooms, sliced
4 cloves garlic, crushed
4 cups water
1 tablespoon liquid smoke flavoring

Directions:
1. Cut the pork roast into large chunks, and season it generously with the Cajun seasoning, brown sugar, and black pepper. Using clean hands, rub the seasoning into the meat, and let it set for 20 minutes.
2. In a deep skillet, melt the butter over medium-high heat. Add the pork, and brown it on all sides. Transfer the meat to a slow cooker.
3. Add the onion, mushrooms, and garlic to the skillet, and cook for a few minutes until tender. Stir in the water, scraping to deglaze all the browned pork bits from the bottom of the pan, then pour the whole mixture into the slow cooker with the pork. Stir in the liquid smoke flavoring.
4. Cover, and cook on high for 6 hours, or until the meat can easily be pulled apart with a fork. Remove the pieces of pork from the slow cooker, and shred them. Return to the liquid in the slow cooker to keep them warm until you are ready to serve.

Barbecue Pulled Pork Sandwiches

Makes 12 servings

Ingredients
1 can beef broth
1 bottle barbecue sauce
3 pounds boneless pork ribs
12 Buns
Favorite toppings such as tomatoes and coleslaw
French fries, for serving

Directions
1. Pour the beef broth into a slow cooker and add the pork ribs. Cook on high heat for 4 hours, until the meat is tender and shreds easily.
2. Preheat the oven to 350°F.
3. Place the shredded pork in a cast iron skillet or Dutch oven and stir in the barbecue sauce.
4. Bake the pork in the oven for 30 minutes until it is properly heated through.
5. Place a generous amount of the pull pork on a bun, top with toppings. Serve with French fries if desired.

Southern Fried Pork Chops

Makes 4 servings

Ingredients
4 thin cut, bone-in pork chops
1 cup buttermilk
Vegetable oil for frying
1 cup self-rising flour
Seasoned salt and pepper to taste

Directions
1. Season each side of the pork with seasoned salt and pepper.
2. Pour the buttermilk into a shallow bowl, and cover a plate or pie pan with flour.
3. Dip the pork chops first onto the buttermilk and then coat with the flour evenly on both sides.
4. Refrigerate for 30 minutes.
5. Heat a few tablespoons of oil in a large pan over high heat, enough to cook four chops at a time.
6. Fry the pork chops, making sure each side is browned, about 8 minutes per side.

Grandma's Beanie Weenies

Serves: 4

Ingredients:
1 (16 ounce) package hot dogs, cut into ¼-inch slices
1 (28 ounce) can baked beans with pork
1 small onion, diced
⅔ cup ketchup
2 tablespoons apple cider vinegar
¼ cup Worcestershire sauce
1 ½ teaspoons garlic powder

Directions:
1. In a large skillet, combine the hot dogs, baked beans, onion, ketchup, cider vinegar, Worcestershire sauce, and garlic powder. Combine well, and bring it to a boil. Reduce the heat to low, cover, and simmer for 25-30 minutes, stirring occasionally.

Old-Country Pork Meatballs

Serves: 6

Ingredients:
1 pound ground pork
½ cup dried bread crumbs
4 large eggs
½ cup whole milk
6 ounces Parmesan, freshly grated
¼ cup sweet onion, minced
2 cloves garlic, minced
2 tablespoons fresh parsley, finely chopped
2 tablespoons fresh basil, finely chopped

Directions:
1. Preheat the oven to 350°F, and prepare a baking sheet with aluminum foil and cooking spray.
2. In a large mixing bowl, combine all the ingredients together, adding more breadcrumbs if the mixture seems too wet.
3. Roll the meatballs out to the size of golf balls, and arrange them on the baking sheet. Bake for 35 to 40 minutes, or until they are no longer pink in the center.

Louisiana Red Bean and Rice

Makes 8 servings

Ingredients
1 pound andouille sausage, sliced
1 pound kidney beans
¼ cup olive oil
1 large onion, chopped
1 green bell pepper, chopped
2 celery stalks, chopped
2 tablespoons garlic, minced
½ teaspoon cayenne pepper
1 tablespoon dried parsley
¼ teaspoon dried sage
1 teaspoon dried thyme
1 teaspoon Cajun seasoning
2 cups long grain white rice
4 cups beef broth
6 cups water
2 bay leaves

Directions
1. Soak the beans in water in a large saucepan overnight.
2. In a medium sized skillet, heat the oil over medium heat, and sauté onion, celery, bell pepper, and garlic in olive oil for 3 to 4 minutes
3. Rinse the beans and cover them with 6 cups of water.
4. Add cooked vegetables to the beans, and stir in the cayenne pepper, parsley, sage, thyme, bay leaves, and Cajun seasoning.
5. Bring the mixture to a boil, and reduce the heat to medium low, and simmer for 2 ½ hours.

6. Stir the sausage into the beans and allow it to simmer for 30 minutes.
7. In a saucepan, boil 4 cups beef broth, and add the rice. Reduce the heat, cover it and allow it to simmer for 20 minutes. You can also use a rice cooker.
8. Serve the bean mixture over the hot rice.

Southern Smothered Pork

Serves: 12

Ingredients:
1 (3 pound) boneless pork loin roast
1 tablespoon Creole seasoning
1 teaspoon salt
½ teaspoon freshly ground black pepper
6 ounces thick cut bacon, diced
⅓ cup all-purpose flour
1 large yellow onion, finely chopped
1 rib celery, finely chopped
½ medium green bell pepper, seeded and chopped
1 tablespoon garlic, minced
6 ounces button mushrooms, thinly sliced
4 cups canned low-sodium beef broth
1 tablespoon Worcestershire sauce
2 tablespoons sliced green onion tops
Cooked white rice, for serving

Directions:
1. Season the roast evenly with Creole seasoning, salt, and black pepper, and with clean hands, rub it into the meat.
2. Heat a Dutch oven and cook the bacon until it is crispy, about 6 minutes. Using a slotted spoon, transfer the bacon to paper towels to drain, and set it aside.
3. Place the roast in the bacon grease in the skillet, and increase the heat to high. Cook until the roast is evenly browned on all sides, about 8-10 minutes. Remove the roast to a plate and cover it loosely with foil.

4. Add the flour to the drippings in the pan and cook, stirring constantly, until a roux the color of milk chocolate is formed, 1-2 minutes. You can add a little butter if the mixture becomes too thick. Add the chopped onion, celery, bell pepper, and cook, stirring, until the vegetables have wilted, about 5 minutes. Stir in the beef broth and Worcestershire sauce.

5. Reduce the heat to low, and place the roast back in the pan. Turn to coat it in the gravy. Cover the pan and cook over low heat, turning occasionally, until an instant-read thermometer inserted into the center of the roast registers 145-150°F, about 45 minutes longer.

6. Remove the roast from the pan and transfer to a platter. Add the green onion tops to the sauce and cook for 10 to 15 minutes, uncovered, until the sauce is thick enough to coat the back of a spoon. Stir the reserved crispy bacon into the sauce, slice the roast and serve, with the sauce ladled over the roast and cooked white rice alongside.

Traditional Meat Pie

Makes 8-10 servings

Ingredients
1 pound ground pork
1 pound ground beef
2 celery stalks, finely diced
1 green bell pepper, chopped
1 large baking potato, peeled and finely chopped
1 bay leaf
1 teaspoon dried thyme leaves
3 cloves of garlic, minced
1 small carrot
1 large onion
1 cup hot water
1 teaspoon Worcestershire sauce
2 beef bouillon cubes
2 tablespoons chopped fresh parsley
Salt free seasoning blend to taste
Salt and pepper to taste
1 egg, separated
2 tablespoons of water
2 sheets frozen puff pastry
2 cups shredded cheddar cheese
Cooking spray

Directions
1. Preheat the oven to 350°F, and coat a 9x13 inch dish with cooking spray.
2. Put a large nonstick skillet over medium high heat and mix the ground pork and beef, cooking until brown and crumbly, about 6-8 minutes. Discard the excess grease.

3. Add the bell pepper, celery, onions and stir, then cover the pan and reduce the heat to medium.
4. Stir frequently, until the vegetables have softened and the onions are translucent, about 4-6 minutes.
5. Make a well in the center of the skillet; place the garlic on the bottom of the pan for a few seconds, and then blend with the meat.
6. Add the parsley, carrot, bay leaf, thyme, potato, Worcestershire sauce, seasoning blend, and salt and pepper to taste.
7. In a bowl, dissolve the bouillon cubes in hot water then pour it into the meat mixture and mix it well. Bring to a boil then reduce the heat from medium to low. Cover and simmer for 10 to 15 minutes until the carrots have softened.
8. In the prepared baking dish, lay one sheet of puff pastry. Gently push the pastry into the corners of the baking dish. Gently spoon the meat mixture into the crust and spread evenly. Avoid adding liquid to the pie as it will cause it to become soggy. Top the mixture with cheddar cheese.
9. In a small bowl, whisk together the egg yolk and a tablespoon of water.
10. Brush the edges of the bottom of the puff pastry sheet.
11. Lay the second sheet of puff pastry on the top and seal the edges by pressing with a fork.
12. Mix the egg white with remaining tablespoon of water, and brush the top surface of the pastry. Poke holes with a fork to vent the crust.
13. Preheat the oven to 350°F and bake the pie until the pastry has turned golden brown. Keep checking your pie after every 15 minutes to prevent your pie from over burning. Serve hot.

Fish and Seafood Recipes

Shrimp and Grits

Makes 6 servings

Ingredients

1 ½ pounds peeled and deveined shrimp

½ teaspoon hot sauce

3 tablespoons fresh lemon juice

2 bacon slices, chopped

½ cup chopped green onions, plus a few tablespoons for serving

1 ½ cup green bell pepper, chopped

1 cup chicken broth

5 cups water

1 tablespoon butter

1 teaspoon salt

1 ½ cups chopped grits

1 ½ teaspoons minced garlic

¾ cup shredded cheddar cheese

Directions

1. In a medium sized bowl, combine the shrimp, hot sauce, and lemon juice.
2. Cook bacon in a skillet over medium heat until nice and crisp.
3. Add ½ cup green onions, bell pepper and garlic to the pan and allow it to cook for 5 minutes until tender, stirring occasionally.
4. Stir in the broth, shrimp mixture, and ¼ cup of green onions, and allow the mixture to cook for 5 minutes, until the shrimp have completely cooked.
5. In another saucepan, bring the water to a boil and then stir in the grits.

6. Lower the heat to low and allow it to simmer, covered, for 5 minutes until the mixture has thickened.
7. Stir in butter and add salt to taste.
8. Serve the shrimp over the grits, with shredded cheese and green onion sprinkled on top.

Classic Crispy Fried Catfish Fillets

Serves: 6

Ingredients:
¾ cup yellow cornmeal
¼ cup all-purpose flour
2 teaspoons salt
1 teaspoon ground black pepper
½ teaspoon garlic powder, to taste
6 (4 ounce) catfish fillets
¼ teaspoon salt
Vegetable oil for frying

Directions:
1. Mix the cornmeal, flour, salt, pepper, and garlic powder in a large shallow dish. Sprinkle the fish with ¼ teaspoon of salt, and dredge it in the cornmeal mixture, turning to coat it evenly.
2. Pour 1 ½ inches of oil into a deep cast-iron skillet and heat it to 350°F. Working in batches, fry the fish for 5 to 6 minutes or until it is golden brown; and drain it on paper towels. Serve hot.

Shrimp Malacca and Rice

Serves: 4

Ingredients:
⅓ cup vegetable oil
2 medium yellow onions, finely diced
1 large green bell pepper, seeded, and finely diced
½ cup celery, strings removed, diced
1 (16 ounce) can whole peeled Italian plum tomatoes
1 cup stewed tomatoes
¼ teaspoon cayenne pepper
¼ teaspoon thyme
2 garlic cloves, minced
2 bay leaves
Salt and freshly ground black pepper
2 tablespoons curry powder
Seafood stock or water
3 pounds shrimp, cleaned and peeled
Cooked white rice

Directions:
1. In a Dutch oven, heat the vegetable oil over medium. Add the onions, bell pepper, and celery, and cook until soft, stirring occasionally.
2. Add the tomatoes, tomato puree, cayenne, thyme, garlic, bay leaves, and salt and black pepper to taste. Increase heat to high, and bring mixture to a boil.
3. Stir in the curry powder. Cover and reduce the heat, and simmer the mixture for about 25 minutes. If the sauce seems too thick, thin it with a little seafood stock or water. Add the shrimp and simmer for about 10 minutes, until just cooked through. Remove the bay leaves.
4. Serve hot, over cooked white rice.

Grandma's Gumbo

Serves: 12

Ingredients:
3-4 pounds small shrimp, cleaned and shelled
1 teaspoon salt
½ teaspoon red pepper flakes
¼ teaspoon garlic powder
1 cup chicken stock
1 cup butter
1 cup flour
2 onions chopped
3 bell peppers, chopped
1 ½ cups celery, chopped
3 teaspoons garlic, minced
3-4 quarts chicken stock
1-1 ½ pounds sliced okra
1 pound kielbasa sausage, cut into ¼-inch slices
5 bay leaves
2 cans stewed tomatoes
1 cup cooked chicken, chopped
5-6 ounces cured ham, chopped
1 bunch fresh parsley, chopped
1 cup chopped green onion (tops only)
1 pound crab meat (or any other seafood, such as clams)
Cooked white rice

Directions:
1. Place shrimp in a large bowl, sprinkle with salt, red pepper, and garlic powder. Stir well, cover, and refrigerate until ready to use.
2. In a large stock pot, melt the butter and stir in the flour. Whisk constantly, until it turns dark, reddish brown. Add the onion, bell peppers, and celery and cook over low heat for about ten minutes, until the vegetables soften. Stir frequently.

3. Stir in the chicken stock.
4. In a skillet, brown the okra and kielbasa, and add it to the stock.
5. Stir in the bay leaves, stewed tomatoes, chicken, and ham. Let this cook about 45 to 90 minutes.
6. Twenty to thirty minutes before serving, add the parsley, green onions, and crab meat. Add the shrimp 5 to 7 minutes before serving, and cook until it is pink.

Crawfish Pie

Makes 6 Servings

Ingredients
¼ cup butter
½ cup celery, chopped
1 cup onion, chopped
½ cup green pepper, chopped
1 ½ teaspoons salt
1 prepared deep dish pie crust, 9 inch
1 cup diced tomatoes
½ teaspoon ground cayenne pepper
2 tablespoons all-purpose flour
1/8 teaspoon white pepper
12 ounces peeled crawfish tails
1 cup water

Directions
1. Line the deep dish pie plate with the pie crust, and set aside.
2. In a large skillet, melt the butter over medium heat, and stir in the celery, onion, green pepper, salt, cayenne pepper, and white pepper, and cook until the vegetables are tender, about 5 minutes.
3. Stir in the tomatoes and the crawfish, reduce the heat, and allow the mixture to cook for 3 minutes to blend the flavors. Stir occasionally.
4. In a large bowl, whisk the flour and water together until smooth, pour the mixture into the skillet.
5. Stir the filling and bring it to a simmer, stirring until the mixture thickens.
6. Remove the mixture from the heat and allow it to rest 20 to 30 minutes
7. Preheat the oven to 400°F.

8. Pour the filling into the prepared pie crust, and bake it in the oven until the crust turns golden brown and the filling starts to bubble, 30 to 40 minutes.
9. Take the pie out of the oven and allow it to cool for 10 minutes before serving.

Tilapia Fillets with Crispy Pecan Coating

Serves: 8

Ingredients:
1 cup milk
½ teaspoon salt
½ teaspoon cayenne powder
1 ½ tablespoons Tabasco sauce
4 tilapia fillets, 6-8 ounces each
2 cups yellow cornmeal
½ cup vegetable oil
½ cup unsalted butter
1 cup chopped pecans
½ cup fresh lemon juice
¾ cup fresh parsley, chopped

Directions:
1. Mix the milk, salt, cayenne powder, and Tabasco sauce in a bowl large enough for all the fillets. Wash the tilapia fillets under cold running water and place them into the milk mixture. Allow them to sit at room temperature for 15-20 minutes.
2. Just before cooking, drain the fillets then roll them in the cornmeal until covered.
3. Heat the vegetable oil in a skillet over medium-high heat. Fry cornmeal-covered fillets until crispy brown (don't crowd the pan), about 2-3 minutes per side. Remove the fish from the pan with a slotted spatula, and drain it on paper towels. Repeat until all the fish is fried. Keep warm.

4. Wipe the skillet with some clean paper towels, and add the butter. Place it over medium heat, and when it has melted, add the nuts. Stir constantly while the pecans brown. Add lemon juice and parsley and stir until well mixed.
5. Spoon the sauce over the tilapia fillets and serve immediately.

Oyster Stew

Makes 4 to 6 servings

Ingredients
1 pint shucked fresh oysters
¼ cup butter
1 shallot, minced
1 clove of garlic, minced
2 tablespoons all-purpose flour
2 cups warm whole or 2% milk
1 cup warm half-and-half cream
1 tablespoon hot sauce
2 tablespoons sherry
1/8 teaspoon celery salt
½ teaspoon Worcestershire sauce
Kosher salt and freshly crack black pepper
Fresh lemon juice
Oyster crackers

Directions
1. Drain the oysters, reserving the oyster liquor.
2. In a small saucepan, heat the oyster liquor and half-and-half over medium heat, stirring continuously for 3 to 4 minutes, until the mixture starts to steam.
3. Add the oysters, cooking for 4 to 5 minutes until the edges of the oysters start to curl.
4. Remove from the heat. With a slotted spoon, transfer the oysters to a plate and reserve.
5. In a large sauce pan, melt the butter, and add garlic and shallot. Cook, stirring occasionally, for 4 minutes until tender.
6. Sprinkle the flour over the mixture and cook, whisking continuously, for 1 to 2 minutes.

7. Slowly add milk, cream, hot sauce, sherry, celery salt, and Worcestershire sauce. Stir until it begins to thicken, then add the oysters.
8. Cook on medium to low heat, stirring occasionally, until it has warmed through.
9. Season the stew with salt and pepper to taste, and serve with a splash of lemon juice and crackers.

Southern Fish Fillets with Sun-dried Tomato Aioli

Serves: 8

Ingredients:
6 (6 ounce) catfish fillets
1 teaspoon salt
½ teaspoon freshly ground pepper
2 cups firmly packed sun dried tomato-flavored pita chips
2 cups all-purpose flour
2 teaspoons Italian seasoning
2 large eggs, lightly beaten
⅓ cup water
Vegetable oil
Sun-dried Tomato Aioli (see recipe below)
Garnishes: fresh basil leaves, lemon slices

Directions:
1. Sprinkle the catfish with salt and pepper.
2. Pulse the pita chips in a food processor 6 to 8 times, or until they are coarsely chopped. Place them in a shallow dish or pie plate suitable for dredging. Stir together the flour and Italian seasoning in another shallow dish or pie plate.
3. Stir together the eggs and ⅓ cup water in a third shallow dish or pie plate.
4. Dredge the catfish in the flour mixture, shaking off any excess. Dip it in the egg mixture, and then the pita chips, pressing the coating into the catfish to coat thoroughly.
5. Pour oil to a depth of 1 inch in a large, deep skillet, and heat it to 350°F. Fry the catfish in batches, 4-5 minutes on each side, or until golden brown. Drain on paper towels.

6. Serve with sun-dried tomato aioli. Garnish with basil and lemon slices, if desired.

For the Sun-dried tomato aioli

7. Blend together 2 small garlic cloves with ⅓ cup sun-dried tomatoes (drained and pat dried) and 1 pinch of cayenne pepper until smooth. Mix-in ½ cup of mayonnaise. Stir to combine.
8. Place in an airtight container in the refrigerator. It will keep for up to 3-4 days.

Grilled Grouper with Watermelon Salsa

Serves: 4

Ingredients:
4 (4 ounce) grouper fillets
1 teaspoon freshly ground pepper
½ teaspoon salt, divided
2 tablespoons olive oil

For the salsa:
2 cups chopped seedless watermelon
¼ cup chopped pitted Kalamata olives
½ English cucumber
1 small jalapeño pepper chopped
2 tablespoons minced red onion
2 tablespoons white balsamic vinegar
½ teaspoon salt
1 tablespoon olive oil

Directions:
1. Preheat the grill to 375°F (medium-high) heat. Sprinkle the grouper with the pepper and ½ teaspoon of the salt. Drizzle with 2 tablespoons olive oil.
2. Grill the fish, covered, for 3-4 minutes on each side or just until it begins to flake when poked with the tip of a sharp knife. It should be opaque in the center.
3. Combine the chopped watermelon, olives, cucumber, jalapeño pepper, red onion, balsamic vinegar, salt and olive oil. Serve with the grilled fish.

Vegetable and Side Recipes
Slow Cooker Red Beans with Rice

Serves: 8
Preparation time: 10 minutes
Cooking time: 7 hours in slow cooker

Ingredients:
1 pound dried red kidney beans
3 slices bacon, chopped
2 cups onion, chopped
1 cup bell pepper, chopped
½ cup celery, chopped
2 cloves garlic, minced
Freshly cracked black pepper, to taste
1 ½ teaspoons dried basil
1 large bay leaf
1 tablespoon vegetable oil
½ pound smoked sausage
1 meaty ham bone or 2 ham hocks
7 cups of hot water
Kosher salt to taste, if needed
Cayenne pepper, to taste, optional
Cooked rice and French bread, for serving

Directions:
1. Rinse and sort the beans, and cover them with cold water in a large saucepan. Bring them to a boil, and simmer for 20 minutes. Drain, and place them in the slow cooker.
2. In a skillet, cook the bacon until the fat is rendered. To that, add the onion, bell pepper, and celery and sauté until the veggies are tender. Add the garlic, black pepper, basil, and bay leaf. Stir it together and transfer it to the slow cooker.

3. Add the oil to the skillet and sauté the sausage until it is nicely browned. Transfer it to the slow cooker, and add the ham bone. If you are using ham hocks, use a knife to cut slashes into the fat before adding them to the slow cooker.
4. Add the 7 cups of hot water, cover, and cook for 5-7 hours on high, or until the beans are tender and cooked through completely.
5. Remove 1 cup of the beans, draining the liquid back into the slow cooker. Mash the beans to form a paste, and stir it back in. Taste, add salt as needed, and cayenne pepper, to taste, if desired.
6. Scoop the beans over hot, cooked rice, and serve with fresh French bread.

Buttermilk Cast Iron Cornbread

Makes 6 servings

Ingredients
2 cups buttermilk
1 cup cornmeal
1 teaspoon baking powder
½ teaspoon baking soda
1 cup flour, all purpose
2 tablespoons white sugar
2 eggs
3 tablespoons butter

Directions
1. Preheat the oven to 375°F.
2. Add the butter to a 10-inch cast iron skillet.
3. Place in the oven while you make the batter.
4. In a large bowl, whisk together the flour, baking soda, and baking powder.
5. Add the cornmeal, and mix until the ingredients are well blended.
6. In a separate bowl, whisk together the eggs and buttermilk.
7. Add the sugar, and blend until the sugar is dissolved.
8. Remove the cast iron skillet from the oven, and tilt the skillet until it is completely coated in butter.
9. Pour the remaining butter into the egg mixture.
10. Add the wet ingredients into the dry, and mix until the batter is smooth.
11. Pour the batter into the cast iron skillet, and place in the oven.
12. Bake for 25 to 30 minutes or until the cornbread golden brown and springs back when pressed.

Granny's Roasted Brussels Sprouts and Mushrooms

Serves: 6

Ingredients:
1 pound Brussels sprouts, trimmed and chopped in bite-sized pieces
1 pound white mushrooms or oyster mushrooms, sliced
Salt and freshly ground pepper
3 tablespoons extra virgin olive oil
1-2 garlic cloves, finely minced
¼ cup finely minced flat-leaf parsley
2 teaspoons lemon zest, minced
2-3 cups quinoa, cooked
½ cup feta or goat cheese, crumbled

Directions:
1. Preheat the oven to 425°F. Line 2 baking sheets or dishes with parchment or foil and, brush them with olive oil.
2. Place the Brussels sprouts on one baking sheet, and the mushrooms on the other. Season with salt and pepper to taste, and drizzle with 1 ½ tablespoons olive oil. Roast both for 20 minutes, stirring halfway through. The Brussels sprouts should be browned on the edges and tender, and the mushrooms should be soft and releasing their juices.
3. Meanwhile, in a small bowl, mix together the garlic, parsley, and lemon zest. Place the mushrooms (with their juices), in a large bowl. Add the Brussels sprouts, and toss them together.
4. Spoon quinoa onto plates or into wide bowls, and top with the Brussels sprouts and mushrooms. Spoon any juices over top, and top with crumbled feta or goat cheese, and serve.

Old Fashioned Creamed Corn

Serves: 4

Ingredients:
3 cups corn whole kernel
2 tablespoons sugar
1 tablespoon all-purpose flour
1 teaspoon salt
½ teaspoon freshly ground black pepper
1 cup heavy cream
½ cup cold water
2 tablespoons bacon grease
1 tablespoon butter

Directions:
1. Scrape the corn kernels into a mixing bowl, together with the milk white juices.
2. Whisk together the sugar, flour, salt, and pepper, and combine the mixture with the corn. Add the heavy cream and water.
3. In a large skillet over medium heat, heat the bacon grease.
4. Add the corn mixture and turn the heat down to medium-low, stirring until it becomes creamy, about 30 minutes. Add the butter right before serving.

Louisiana Green Bean Casserole

Serves: 6

Ingredients:
2 tablespoons butter
2 tablespoons all-purpose flour
1 teaspoon salt
½ teaspoon black pepper
1 teaspoon white sugar
½ cup onion, diced
1 cup sour cream
7 cups fresh green beans, cooked and drained

<u>For the topping:</u>
½ cups shredded Cheddar cheese
½ cup crumbled buttery round crackers
1 tablespoon butter, melted

Directions:
1. Preheat the oven to 350°F.
2. Melt the butter in a large skillet over medium heat. Stir in the flour until smooth, and cook for one minute. Stir in the salt, pepper, sugar, onion, and sour cream. Add the green beans, and stir to coat.
3. Transfer the mixture to a 2 ½ quart casserole dish. Spread the shredded cheese over the top. In a small bowl, stir together the cracker crumbs and remaining butter, and sprinkle this mixture over the cheese.
4. Bake the casserole for 30 minutes, or until the top is golden and the cheese is bubbly.

Old South Creamy Coleslaw

Makes 8 Servings

Ingredients
1 head cabbage, finely shredded
2 carrots, finely chopped
2 tablespoons finely chopped onion
⅓ cup white sugar
¼ cup buttermilk
2 tablespoons lemon juice
2 tablespoons distilled white vinegar
½ teaspoon salt
1/8 teaspoon ground black pepper

Directions
1. In a large salad bowl, mix together carrots, onions, and cabbage.
2. In a separate bowl, whisk sugar, buttermilk, lemon juice, vinegar, and salt and pepper until the mixture is smooth and the sugar has dissolved.
3. Pour the dressing onto the cabbage mixture.
4. Cover the bowl and refrigerate for at least 2 hours.
5. Mix coleslaw again before serving.

Pinto Beans

Makes 8 to 10 servings

Ingredients
2 cups dried pinto beans
4 cups of chicken broth
¼ pound cooked ham, shredded
1 teaspoon black pepper
½ teaspoon thyme
2 teaspoons salt
½ teaspoon garlic powder
½ teaspoon dried oregano
¼ teaspoon chili powder
¼ teaspoon ground cumin
3 bay leaves

Directions
1. Soak the beans in water overnight, or for at least 6 to 8 hours
2. The following day, drain the beans and discard the water, and place the beans in a slow cooker with all the other ingredients.
3. Cook the mixture on low for 10 hours, or on high for 5 hours
4. After the mixture has finished cooking, take 2 cups of the bean soup and puree, using a food processor or blender.
5. Add the puree back to the beans, and cook on high for at least 30 minutes. This will thicken the soup.
6. Remove the beans from the slow cooker and serve.

Cheesy Smooth Mashed Potatoes

Makes 10 servings

Ingredients
2 packages of cream cheese (3 ounces each)
5 pounds baking potatoes
1 container of sour cream (8 ounces)
2 teaspoons onion salt
½ cup butter or margarine
½ cup milk
Parsley, to garnish
Cooking spray

Directions
1. Preheat the oven to 325°F.
2. Peel potatoes and cut them into 1 inch cubes.
3. Bring a large pot of water to a boil, and cook the potatoes for 15 to 20 minutes until tender.
4. Drain the potatoes and place them in a large mixing bowl.
5. Add the cream cheese, sour cream, margarine, milk, and onion salt, and beat all the ingredients at medium speed with electric mixer until smooth and fluffy.
6. Greased a 3-quart baking dish with cooking spray. Spoon in the potatoes mixture, and bake for 10 minutes until heated through.
7. Garnish with parsley and serve.

Country Cabbage and Bacon

Serves: 4

Ingredients:
3 slices bacon, cut into thirds
⅓ cup butter
1 teaspoon salt
1 teaspoon ground black pepper
1 head cabbage, cored and sliced
1 white onion, chopped
½ teaspoon white sugar

Directions:
1. Place the bacon and butter in a Dutch oven over medium heat. Season with salt and pepper.
2. Cook for about 5 minutes, or until the bacon is crisp.
3. Without draining the fat, add the cabbage, onion, and sugar to the pot. Cook and stir continuously for 5 minutes, until tender.

Southern Biscuits

Serves: 8

Ingredients:
2 cups flour
4 teaspoons baking powder
½ teaspoon baking soda
¾ teaspoon salt
2 tablespoons butter, cold
2 tablespoons shortening
1 cup buttermilk, chilled

Directions:
1. Preheat the oven to 450°F.
2. In a large mixing bowl, combine flour, baking powder, baking soda, and salt. Using your clean fingertips, rub butter and shortening into the dry ingredients until mixture is uniformly crumbly.
3. Make a well in the center, and pour in the buttermilk. Stir just until the dough comes together, it will be very sticky.
4. Turn the dough out onto a floured surface, dust the top with flour, and gently fold the dough over on itself 5-6 times. Press it into a 1-inch thick circle. Using a 2-ince circular cutter, cut out the biscuits, being sure to push straight down through the dough and then pull the cutter straight back up without turning it side to side.
5. Place the biscuits on a baking sheet so that they just touch. Reform the remaining dough into a circle, working it as little as possible, and continue cutting biscuits until it is all used up.
6. Bake until the biscuits are tall and light gold on top, 15-20 minutes.

Fried Okra

Makes 4 servings

Ingredients
10 pods of okra
1 cup cornmeal
¼ teaspoon ground pepper
½ cup vegetable oil
¼ teaspoon salt
1 egg
Kosher salt and white pepper vinegar, for serving

Directions
1. Beat the egg in a large bowl, and soak the okra in it for 10 minutes.
2. In another, medium sized bowl, combine salt, pepper, and cornmeal.
3. Heat oil in a large skillet over medium high heat.
4. Dip the okra in the cornmeal mixture, coating it evenly on all sides.
5. Place okra in the hot oil, reduce the heat to medium low as the okra starts to turn brown. Stir continuously.
6. Drain on paper towels, and serve with salt and pepper vinegar.

Southern Braised Red Cabbage

Serves: 4

Ingredients:
½ baguette, split
4 tablespoons butter, divided
Pinch of paprika
½ teaspoon sea salt
One 1-1 ½ pound head red cabbage, quartered, cored and thinly sliced (about 8 cups)
1 sprig fresh rosemary, finely chopped
1 teaspoon white sugar
¼ teaspoon salt
2-4 tablespoons apple cider vinegar

Directions:
1. With your fingertips, separate the soft center of the baguette from the crust and pull it apart into small pieces. Set aside the crust for another use.
2. In a sauté pan, melt 2 tablespoons of the butter over medium heat. When the butter is very hot, add the breadcrumbs and cook, stirring constantly, until they are dark golden brown and crunchy, 7-10 minutes. Stir in the paprika and salt. Transfer the breadcrumbs to a plate lined with paper towel, and set them aside.
3. In a heavy-bottomed skillet or Dutch oven, melt the remaining 2 tablespoons of butter over medium heat. Add the cabbage, rosemary, sugar, and salt. Cook, stirring occasionally, until the cabbage starts to wilt, about 5 minutes.

4. Add the cider, stir, and cover, and cook until the liquid evaporates, about 15 minutes. Stir constantly until the cabbage is completely tender, about 3 minutes.
5. Season to taste, adding more apple cider vinegar if desired, and top with the sautéed breadcrumbs. Serve immediately.

Sautéed Collard Greens

Serves: 4

Ingredients:
12 hickory smoked bacon slices, finely chopped
2 medium sweet onions, finely chopped
¾ pound smoked ham, chopped
6 cloves garlic, finely chopped
3 quarts chicken broth
3 pounds fresh collard greens, washed and trimmed
⅓ cup apple cider vinegar
1 tablespoon sugar
1 teaspoon salt
3/4 teaspoon pepper

Directions:
1. In a large stock pot over medium heat, cook the bacon for 10 minutes, or until it is almost crisp.
2. Add the onion, and sauté 8 minutes, until it is translucent. Stir in the ham and garlic, and sauté 1 minute.
3. Stir in the broth and the remaining ingredients. Cook for 2 hours, or until the greens are tender.

Fresh Corn Cakes

Makes 3 dozens

Ingredients
3 large eggs
¾ cup milk
1 cup fresh corn kernels
¾ cup all-purpose flour
3 tablespoons melted butter
¾ cup yellow or white cornmeal
2 tablespoons chopped fresh chives
1 8-ounces package fresh mozzarella cheese, grated
1 teaspoon salt
1 teaspoon ground pepper
Chives for serving

Directions
1. Pulse the corn, eggs, milk, and butter in a food processor 3 to 4 times until the corn is coarsely chopped.
2. Combine the flour, cornmeal, cheese, chives, and salt and pepper together in a large bowl. Stir in the corn mixture until the dry ingredients are moistened.
3. Spoon 1/8 cup batter for each cake onto a greased non-stick pan.
4. Cook the cakes for 2 to 3 minutes per side until browned.
5. Garnish with chopped chives and serve.

Pickled Green Tomatoes

Makes 6 pints

Ingredients
5 pounds green tomatoes, chopped
2 tablespoons pickling salt
1 large onion, chopped
2 cups cider vinegar
1 ½ cups firmly packed brown sugar
2 teaspoons celery seed
2 teaspoons whole allspice
2 teaspoons mustard seeds
½ teaspoon whole cloves
3 cups water

Directions
1. Season the tomatoes and onions with pickling salt, and let it stand for 4 to 7 hours.
2. Drain the ingredients and pat dry with paper towels, set aside.
3. In a Dutch oven, combine vinegar and brown sugar, and cook over medium heat. Stir the constantly until the brown sugar dissolves.
4. Place the celery seed, allspice, mustard seeds, and whole cloves in a 6 inch square of cheese cloth, and tie it with a string.
5. Add the spice bag, along with the tomatoes, onions, and 3 cups of water to the vinegar mixture.
6. Bring the ingredients to a boil, stirring constantly. Reduce the heat and allow the mixture to simmer, stirring occasionally, for 25 minutes, until the onions and tomatoes are tender.
7. Remove and discard the spice bag.

8. Pour the hot pickles into mason jars, tap the jars to remove any air bubbles and cover the jar with the metal lid.
9. Process in boiling water bath for at least 10 minutes.

Summer Squash Casserole

Makes 8 to 10 servings

Ingredients

2 pounds yellow summer squash
1 large onion, chopped
7 tablespoons butter, divided
1 large clove garlic, chopped
½ green bell pepper, chopped
½ red bell pepper, chopped
4 slices plain white bread, toasted
1 jalapeño pepper, seeded and chopped
24 round buttery crackers, crumbled in a food processor
½ cup heavy whipping cream
½ pound sharp cheddar cheese
1 teaspoon salt
1 teaspoon sugar
4 large eggs, beaten
¼ teaspoon cayenne pepper

Directions

1. Heat the oven to 350°F, and grease a 2-quart baking dish with butter.
2. Cut the squash to ½ inch thick slices, and boil in salted water for 10 minutes, until cooked through.
3. Drain the squash, and purée in a food processor.
4. Over medium heat, melt 6 tablespoon of butter, add onion, peppers and garlic, and cook until the mixture is tender.
5. In the meantime, put the toast in a food processor, melt the remaining butter and combine it with the crumbs.

6. Combine the squash puree, garlic, crackers, cheese, peppers, and onion together, and mix well. Stir in the sugar, cream, egg and seasonings, and blend.
7. Pour the mixture in a baking dish.
8. Top it with toast crumbs, and bake for 40 minutes until browned.

Macaroni and Cheese

Serves 6-8

Ingredients

8 ounces dried elbow macaroni (you can also use whole wheat pasta if desired)
1/2 cup bread crumbs
¾ cups whole milk
¼ cup all-purpose flour
¼ cup butter, melted
1 cup sharp cheddar cheese + ½ cup for topping, shredded
1 cup Monterey jack cheese, shredded
1 cup processed cheddar cheese, cut into small cubes
1 pinch cayenne pepper
½ teaspoon paprika
Kosher salt and freshly ground pepper
Butter

Directions

1. Pre-heat the oven to 350ºF.
2. Bring large pot of water to boil, add salt and cook pasta according to package instructions. Drain the macaroni in a strainer. Rinse under cold running water and drain to stop the cooking process.
3. Toss bread crumbs and melted butter to coat. Set aside
4. Generously butter a baking dish.
5. In a large mixing bowl, add all the ingredients EXCEPT the bread crumb mixture, and stir to combine. Transfer to the buttered casserole baking dish. Top with the bread crumbs mixture and cheddar cheese.
6. Place baking dish on baking sheet. Bake until bubbling, and cheesy top is golden brown, about 40-45 minutes. Let cool 5 minutes before serving.

Grilled Sweet Potato Wedges

Serves: 6

Ingredients:

4 medium sweet potatoes, cut into wedges (approximately 6-8 wedges each)
2 tablespoons olive oil
1 teaspoon paprika
1 teaspoon garlic powder
¼ teaspoon cinnamon
¼ teaspoon cayenne powder
¼ teaspoon salt

Directions:

1. Prepare and ignite your grill. Place grate over medium temperature heat source and allow to preheat for at least 5 minutes.
2. In a large bowl, toss the sweet potato wedges with the olive oil.
3. In a small bowl, combine the paprika, garlic powder, cinnamon, cayenne powder, and salt. Sprinkle seasoning over wedges until all wedges are well seasoned.
4. Place sweet potato wedges on grill grate, trying to avoid setting them on the hottest areas. Grill potatoes until firm tender, approximately 35 minutes, turning occasionally to ensure even doneness. Transfer grilled wedges to the hottest part of the grate for a final crisping. Grill for one to minutes.
5. Remove from heat and serve immediately

Okra and Pecan Casserole

Makes 6 to 7 servings

Ingredients
1 cup pecans
1 teaspoon salt
1 ½ cup all-purpose baking mix
½ teaspoon pepper
2 packages of frozen whole okra (10-ounce each)
Peanut oil for frying

Directions
1. In a shallow pan, spread pecans in an single layer
2. Bake at 350°F for 10 minutes, until they are lightly toasted, stirring occasionally.
3. Process pecans, baking mix, salt, and pepper in a food processer until the pecans are finely ground.
4. In a large bowl, toss the okra and the pecan mixture to coat.
5. Pour oil into a Dutch oven, heating it to 350°F.
6. Fry the okra in batches until they are golden brown, 5 to 6 minutes
7. Drain on paper towels and serve.

Creamy Tri-color Corn

Makes 8 servings

Ingredients
6 cups fresh corn kernels
8 bacon slices
1 cup sweet onions, diced
½ cup green pepper, chopped
½ cup red pepper, chopped
1 package cream cheese (8 ounces)
1 teaspoon sugar
1 teaspoon salt
1 teaspoon pepper
½ cup half and half

Directions
1. In a large skillet, cook the bacon over medium high heat for 6 to 8 minutes until crispy.
2. Drain the bacon on paper towels, reserving about 2 tablespoons of drippings in the skillet. Coarsely crumble the bacon.
3. Sauté the corn, bell peppers and sweet onion over medium high heat for 6 minutes until tender.
4. Add cream cheese and half and half, stir the mixture until the cheese melts.
5. Stir in the sugar, salt, and pepper.
6. Transfer to a serving dish, and top with bacon.

Dessert Recipes

Southern Pecan Pie

Serves: 8

Ingredients:
1 cup sugar
1 ½ cups corn syrup (dark, light, or a combination)
4 eggs
¼ cup butter
1 ½ teaspoons vanilla
½ teaspoon salt
1 ½ cups pecans, coarsely broken
1 unbaked deep dish pie shell

Directions:
1. Preheat the oven to 350°F.
2. In medium saucepan, boil the sugar and corn syrup together for 2-3 minutes, and set aside to cool slightly.
3. In large bowl, beat the eggs lightly, and then very slowly pour the syrup mixture into the eggs, stirring constantly.
4. Strain the mixture to make sure there are no lumps. Stir in the butter, vanilla, salt, and pecans and pour into crust.
5. Bake for about 45 to 60 minutes, or until set.

Peach Ice Cream

Makes 24 servings

Ingredients
4 cups peeled peaches, diced
1 cup sugar
1 can sweetened condensed milk (14-ounce)
1 package vanilla instant pudding mix (3.75-ounce)
1 can evaporated milk (12-ounce)
4 cups half and half

Directions
1. Combine the peaches and sugar together, and let stand for an hour.
2. Process in a food processor until smooth.
3. In a large bowl, stir together the evaporated milk and pudding mix, then add the peach puree, half and half, and condensed milk
4. Pour this mixture into an ice cream maker, and follow the manufacturer's instructions.

Grandma's Caramel Layer Cake

Serves: 6

Ingredients:

For the cake:

1 cup unsalted butter, at room temperature

⅓ cup vegetable oil

2 ½ cups granulated sugar

6 large eggs, plus 2 egg yolks, room temperature

2 tablespoons vanilla extract

3 cups cake flour, sifted

1 teaspoon baking powder

½ teaspoon salt

1 cup sour cream

For the icing:

1 ½ sticks butter

2 (12 ounce) cans evaporated milk

2 cups granulated sugar

2 teaspoons pure vanilla extract

Directions:

1. Preheat the oven to 350°F.
2. In a large mixing bowl, the cream butter, oil and sugar on high speed until they are light and fluffy, about 5-6 minutes.
3. Turn mixer to medium and, one at a time, add the eggs and egg yolks, mixing after each until it is until well incorporated.
4. Add the vanilla extract and mix.

5. In a separate bowl, sift the cake flour, baking powder, and salt. With the mixer on low speed, alternate adding flour mixture and sour cream ending, with flour mixture, mixing to be sure each addition is fully incorporated before adding more.
6. Spray three 9-inch round cake pans with baking spray, and divide the batter among them.
7. Bake for 23-30 minutes or until a toothpick inserted in the center comes out clean. Cool the cakes on racks for 10 minutes before removing them from the pans. Wait until they are completely cooled before frosting them.

For the Caramel Icing:

8. Combine the butter, evaporated milk, and sugar in a saucepan over medium heat until everything has melted together.
9. Continue cooking over low to medium heat for 1 ½-2 hours, stirring periodically. Be careful that it does not burn. It will thicken and darken to a beautiful golden brown. It should also thickly coat the back of a spoon.
10. Remove the pot from the heat and add the vanilla extract. Cool for about 15-20 minutes to allow it to thicken before icing the cake.

Aunt Sarah's Strawberry Shortcake

Makes 8-12 servings

Ingredients
2 pounds fresh strawberries, hulled and quartered
¾ cup sugar, divided
¾ cup cold butter
2 large eggs
1 cup whipping cream
¼ teaspoon almond extract
1 container sour cream (8 ounces)
1 teaspoon vanilla extract
4 teaspoon baking powder
2 ¾ cups all-purpose flour
2 tablespoons sugar

Directions
1. Combine together the strawberries, ½ cup sugar, and almond extract. Cover the mixture and allow it to rest for 10 minutes.
2. At a medium speed, beat the whipping cream with an electric mixture until foamy.
3. Slowly add 2 tablespoons of sugar, beating until soft peaks start to form. Cover the mixture and keep refrigerated until ready to use.
4. Preheat the oven to 450°F.
5. Combine together the flour, remaining ¼ cup sugar and baking powder in a large bowl. Cut the butter into the flour mixture with pastry blender until crumbly.
6. In another bowl, whisk together sour cream, eggs, and vanilla until well blended, then add to the flour mixture and stir until all the dry ingredients are moistened.

7. Drop dough by lightly greased ⅓ cupful onto a lightly greased baking sheet, and bake for 12 to 15 minutes until golden.
8. Cut the shortcakes in half horizontally, and spoon ½ cup of the berry mixture and scoop it on the bottom of the short cake, top with a tablespoon of whipped cream, cover the top and serve with the remaining whipped cream.

Classic Key Lime Pie

Makes 1 pie - 8 servings

Ingredients
<u>Crust</u>
¼ cup firmly packed light brown sugar
1 ¼ cups graham cracker crumbs
⅓ cup butter, melted
<u>Filling</u>
1. can sweetened condensed milk (14-ounce)
⅔ fresh lime juice
2 teaspoons lime zest
3 egg yolks
<u>Topping</u>
2 egg whites, at room temperature
2 tablespoons granulated sugar
¼ teaspoon cream of tartar

Directions
1. Preheat the oven at 350°F and place oven rack in middle position.
2. Combine the cracker crumbs, brown sugar, and melted butter in a 9-inch pie plate and press gently to form a crust.
3. Bake for 10 to 15 minutes until it is lightly brown, allow it to cool.
4. Beat the egg yolks until fluffy and light yellow in color, about 4-5 minutes on high speed. Slowly add the condensed milk, lime juice, and lime zest. Beat until fluffy, about 4-5 more minutes.
5. Pour filling in cooled graham crust. Set aside.
6. With an electric mixer, beat the egg whites and cream of tartar at high speed until foamy.

7. Gradually add the granulated sugar, 1 tablespoon at a time, and beat the mixture until soft peaks start to appear and the sugar is all dissolved.
8. Spread this meringue over the prepared pie filling.
9. Bake the pie into the oven at 325°F for 25 to 28 minutes.
10. Let cool down and place in the refrigerator 2-3 hours before serving.

Note: using key limes for the lime juice gives this pie an authentic flavor like no others.

Best Ever Coconut Layered Cake

Makes 8-12 servings

Ingredients
3 cups all-purpose flour
2 2/3 cups sugar
5 large eggs
1 package frozen flaked coconut (6 ounces)
1 ½ cups butter, softened
1 teaspoon vanilla extract
½ teaspoon salt
1 cup milk
1 teaspoon baking powder
1 cup coconut shavings
2 teaspoon baking powder

Coconut Filling
¼ cup powdered sugar
2 cups whipping cream
½ cup coconut flakes
1 teaspoon coconut extract
1 teaspoon vanilla extract

Directions
1. Preheat the oven to 400°F.
2. Beat the flour, sugar, butter, milk, baking powder, and salt together at medium speed with an electric mixer until well blended.
3. Add the extracts and blend well.
4. Gradually start adding the eggs, one at a time, beating until all the ingredients are blended.
5. Stir in the flaked coconut, and pour the batter in to 4 individual cake pans.

6. Bake the cakes for 20 minutes, and then cool on wire racks 10 minutes before removing them from the pans.
7. Reduce the oven temperature to 350°F and bake the coconut shavings in a single layer in a shallow pan, for 10 minutes or until toasted, stirring occasionally. Set the toasted coconut aside.
8. Beat whipping cream on high speed until foamy, and slowly add the coconut and vanilla extracts, coconut flakes and powdered sugar, beating the mixture until soft peaks start to foam.
9. When the cakes have cooled, prepare the coconut filling and spread it between the layers.
10. Spread the remaining frosting on the top and sides of the cake, and carefully press toasted coconut into the frosting.
11. Keep chilled until ready to serve.

Red Velvet Cake

Makes 8-12 servings

Ingredients
2 teaspoons fine salt
2 ¾ cups plus 1 tablespoon sifted cake flour
2 teaspoons baking powder
2 tablespoons red food coloring
¼ teaspoon baking soda
1 ½ tablespoons water
2 sticks unsalted butter, softened, plus some more for greasing pans
1 ½ teaspoons vanilla extract
2 cups granulated sugar
¼ cup unsweetened cocoa powder
3 large eggs
1 tablespoon finely grated orange zest
1 cup whole or low fat buttermilk

For Icing
1 pound sifted powdered sugar (4 cups)
1 ½ sticks unsalted butter (¾ cup)
1 pound cream cheese
2 tablespoons whole milk

Directions
1. Heat the oven to 350°F, and grease a 9-inch cake pan with butter, then flour. Tap off the excess flour, and set aside.
2. Sift the baking powder, baking soda, flour, and salt twice together, set aside.
3. Whisk the water, cocoa, vanilla, and food coloring in a small bowl until smooth, set aside.

4. In a large bowl, beat the butter on medium speed with an electric mixer until creamy, about 30 seconds. Add the sugar, ¼ cup at a time, beating about 15 minutes, until the mixture becomes fluffy.
5. Gradually add the eggs one at a time, along with the orange zest, beating after each addition. Add the red cocoa mix.
6. On low speed, alternately add the flour mixture and the buttermilk, starting and ending with the flour mixture. Beat the batter using a spatula, 10 to 12 strokes.
7. Divide cake batter into two cake pans, and bake for 30 minutes, or until a toothpick inserted in the center comes out clean.
8. Remove the cakes from the oven and allow the cakes to rest for 10 minutes before removing from the pans.
9. In the meantime, prepare the icing. In a large bowl, mix all the ingredients together at high speed, gradually reduce the speed until light and fluffy.
10. When the cakes are completely cool, place 1 cake on a serving plate. Spread the icing on the top. Place second cake on top and spread icing on top and sides.

Mississippi Mud Pie

Makes 1 pie - 8-12 servings

Ingredients
¼ cup sugar
1 package cream cheese (8 ounces)
¾ cup sugar
2 cups graham cracker crumbs
3 cups milk
1 package instant chocolate pudding mix (3 ½ ounce)
1 package instant butter scotch pudding mix (3 ½ ounce)
1 container whipped topping

Directions
1. Combine together the graham cracker crumbs with ¼ cup sugar and butter, and press firmly into a large pie plate.
2. Blend the cream cheese and sugar until smooth, and spread on the prepared crust.
3. In a separate bowl, mix together the pudding mixes and the milk until well blended and spread this on top of the cream cheese mixture.
4. Top with whipped topping.
5. Chill the pie.

Old-Fashioned Buttermilk Pie

Serves: 8

Ingredients:
½ cup butter, melted
1 ½ cups sugar
3 tablespoons flour
3 eggs, beaten
1 pinch salt
1 pinch nutmeg
1 teaspoon vanilla
1 cup buttermilk
1 prepared deep dish pie shell

Directions:
1. Preheat the oven to 400°F.
2. With an electric mixer on medium speed, beat the butter and sugar together until light. Add the eggs one at a time and continue beating until fully incorporated, then mix in the vanilla.
3. In a separate bowl, sift the dry ingredients together. Alternating with the buttermilk, add them in increments to the batter. Beat until smooth.
4. Pour the mixture into the pie shell and bake for 10 minutes. Reduce the heat to 350°F and bake for an additional 50-60 minutes, or until a clean knife inserted in the center comes out clean.

Granny's Fried Apple Pocket Pies

Serves: 24

Ingredients:

4 (6 ounce) bags dried apples
2 cups granulated sugar
4 heaping cups self-rising flour
1 cup butter
1 ½-2 cups ice water
Additional flour for mixing dough
1 ½ cups shortening, divided

Directions:

For the apples

1. Place the apples in a large pot or Dutch oven, and add enough water to almost cover them. Stir in the sugar. Bring them to a boil over medium-high heat.
2. Lower the heat so the apples continue to simmer.
3. Break up the apples with a wooden spoon as they cook. Simmer until they are tender and juicy, stirring frequently. You may need to add more water as they cook. Remove them from the heat and let them cool down.

For the dough

4. Start with 4 heaping cups of self-rising flour and cut in the butter with a fork or your fingers. Mix well until the butter is incorporated into the flour.
5. Add 1 ½ cups of ice water to the flour mixture, and more as needed to get all the dry flour mixed in. Mix with a fork until the dough is sticky. Dip your hands in flour and sprinkle additional flour onto dough so you can knead it, and knead the dough until it is smooth and not sticky.

6. Set it aside to rest for ten minutes.
7. Pinch off pieces of dough to make balls slightly smaller than ping pong balls. Roll each ball out into a thin circle.
8. Add a heaping spoonful or two of apples to one side of rolled dough. (You will learn from experience exactly how much of the apple mixture to use.) The dough should fold over without tearing, leaving you with a plump pie.
9. Dip your finger in water and rub it around the edges of the dough. Carefully fold the dough over and press the edges together lightly to seal. Using a fork, crimp the edges.
10. Prepare a large tray or pan with a few layers of paper towel.
11. Once all the pies are ready, melt about ½ cup of shortening a large skillet heat over medium-high heat.
12. When a drop of water sizzles in the grease, it is hot enough to begin. Carefully lay 2 or 3 pies in the skillet.
13. Cook for about 1-1 ½ minutes on each side, until they are golden brown. Set them aside to drain and cool slightly, and then serve. The pies will keep for a few days, but are best when eaten promptly.

Southern Style Chocolate Cake

Serves: 8

Ingredients:
1 cup butter
1 cup water
4 tablespoons unsweetened cocoa powder
½ cup buttermilk
1 teaspoon baking soda
2 eggs, beaten
1 ½ teaspoons vanilla extract
2 cups all-purpose flour
2 cups white sugar
1 teaspoon ground cinnamon
1 teaspoon salt

<u>For the icing</u>
½ cup butter
4 tablespoons unsweetened cocoa powder
⅓ cup buttermilk
4 cups icing sugar
1 teaspoon vanilla extract
1 cup chopped pecans
1 pinch salt

Directions
1. Preheat the oven to 350°F. Grease and flour a 9x13 pan.
2. In a saucepan, melt the butter. Stir in the water and cocoa powder until smooth. Remove the pot from the heat and set it aside.
3. In a medium bowl, dissolve the baking soda in the buttermilk. Whisk in the eggs and vanilla, and the cooled cocoa mixture.

4. In a separate, large bowl, sift together the flour, sugar, cinnamon, and salt. Make a well in the center and pour in the cocoa buttermilk mixture. Stir until blended, but do not overmix.
5. Pour the batter into the prepared pan. Bake for 30 minutes, or until a toothpick inserted into the center of the cake comes out clean.
6. Prepare the icing. In a large saucepan, melt the butter and mix in the cocoa. Stir in the buttermilk, and heat it until it is almost boiling.
7. Stir in the icing sugar, vanilla, pecans, and salt. Remove it from the heat. Mix well and pour it over the cake while it is still warm.

Old-Fashioned Lemon Bars

Serves: 12

Ingredients:

2 cups all-purpose flour
1 teaspoon baking soda
1 teaspoon ground cinnamon
½ teaspoon ground nutmeg
½ teaspoon salt
¾ cup butter
1 ½ cups packed brown sugar
2 eggs
3 tablespoons fresh lemon juice
3 tablespoons lemon zest
1 cup raisins

Directions:

1. Preheat the oven to 350°F, and lightly grease a 9-inch square baking pan.
2. In a medium bowl, combine the flour, baking soda, cinnamon, nutmeg, and salt, and set aside.
3. In a large bowl, cream together the butter and brown sugar. Beat in the eggs one at a time, mixing until well incorporated.
4. Add the lemon juice and zest, and gradually blend in the dry ingredients. Stir in the raisins, and spread the batter evenly in the prepared baking pan.
5. Bake for 30 minutes, or until set and browned at the edges.

Southern Tea Cakes

Serves: 6

Ingredients:
1 cup butter, softened
1 ½ cups sugar
1 ½ teaspoons vanilla
1 egg
⅓ cup buttermilk
1 teaspoon baking soda, dissolved in milk
3 ½ cups self-rising flour

Directions:
1. Preheat the oven to 350° F, and line rimmed baking sheet with parchment paper or a silicon baking mat.
2. Cream the butter and sugar together until light and fluffy, about 3 minutes. Add the vanilla and egg, and mix to combine.
3. In a glass measuring cup, stir the buttermilk and baking soda together, and add them to mixture, alternately with the flour.
4. Lightly flour a clean work surface, and roll the dough out to 1-inch thickness.
5. Cut out the biscuits with a cutter, and place them on the prepared baking pan. Bake until lightly browned, about 12-15 minutes.

Pineapple Cake with Coco-Pecan Frosting

Serves: 8

Ingredients:

For the cake:
1 ½ cups sugar
2 teaspoon baking soda
2 cups flour
½ teaspoon salt
2 eggs
1 (15 ½ ounce) can crushed pineapple
1 teaspoon vanilla

For the frosting:
1 ½ cups sugar
½ cup butter, softened
1 (5 ounce) can evaporated milk
1 c. pecans, chopped
Pinch of salt
1 ½ cups coconut
1 teaspoon vanilla

Directions:

1. Preheat the oven to 350°F, and prepare a 9x13 pan with cooking spray.
2. Mix the dry ingredients together in a large bowl. Stir in the beaten eggs, pineapple, and vanilla. Beat well and pour it into the pan.
3. Bake for 40 minutes, or until the edges pull away from the pan and a toothpick inserted in the center comes out clean.
4. To make the frosting, put all the ingredients into large saucepan and bring them to a boil. Boil for 6 minutes, and pour it over the cake while the cake is still warm.

Chewy Peanut Date Bars

Serves: 18

Ingredients:
½ cup honey
¼ cup peanut butter
1 tablespoon butter
1 teaspoon vanilla
½ teaspoon ground cinnamon
Pinch nutmeg
2 cups rice or oat cereal
⅔ cup golden raisins, or dried cranberries
½ cup dry roasted peanuts or chopped pecans

Directions:
1. Prepare a 9-inch square baking pan with cooking spray.
2. In large saucepan, combine the honey, peanut butter, and butter. Stir over medium heat until the mixture is melted and well blended.
3. Remove the pot from the heat, and stir in vanilla and cinnamon.
4. Stir in cereal, raisins, and peanuts. (For a change, try dried cranberries or chopped apricots instead of raisins.)
5. Firmly press the mixture into the baking pan. Let it cool, and cut it into bars. Store covered, in the refrigerator.

Old South Sugar Cake

Serves: 8

Ingredients:
1 cup whole milk
½ cup pure vegetable shortening
1 vanilla bean, scrapped insides only
1 teaspoon hazelnut extract
2 cups flour
1 ½ cup white sugar
1 tablespoon baking powder
¾ teaspoon salt
4 egg whites
¼ cup powdered sugar
1 cup fresh blackberries

Directions:
1. Preheat the oven to 350°F and lightly oil a 10 inch cast iron skillet.
2. Combine the milk, vegetable shortening, vanilla and hazelnut extract. Cream together until smooth.
3. In a separate bowl combine the flour, sugar, baking powder and salt. Add the dry ingredients to the wet ingredients in two or three increments, mixing just until blended.
4. Add the egg whites and mix until blended.
5. Pour the batter into the cast iron skillet and lightly tap to even out and remove large air bubbles.
6. Place the skillet in the oven and bake for 40 minutes, or until cooked in the center.
7. Remove from the oven and let cool slightly before sprinkling with powdered sugar.
8. Serve directly out of the skillet with fresh blackberries.

Appendix - Cooking Conversion Charts

1. Measuring Equivalent Chart

Type	Imperial	Imperial	Metric
Weight	1 dry ounce		28g
	1 pound	16 dry ounces	0.45 kg
Volume	1 teaspoon		5 ml
	1 dessert spoon	2 teaspoons	10 ml
	1 tablespoon	3 teaspoons	15 ml
	1 Australian tablespoon	4 teaspoons	20 ml
	1 fluid ounce	2 tablespoons	30 ml
	1 cup	16 tablespoons	240 ml
	1 cup	8 fluid ounces	240 ml
	1 pint	2 cups	470 ml
	1 quart	2 pints	0.95 l
	1 gallon	4 quarts	3.8 l
Length	1 inch		2.54 cm

*   Numbers are rounded to the closest equivalent

2. Oven Temperature Equivalent Chart

T(°F)	T(°C)
220	100
225	110
250	120
275	140
300	150
325	160
350	180
375	190
400	200
425	220
450	230
475	250
500	260

* $T(°C) = [T(°F)-32] * 5/9$

** $T(°F) = T(°C) * 9/5 + 32$

*** Numbers are rounded to the closest equivalent

Made in the USA
Middletown, DE
24 October 2017